True North

A FLICKERING SOUL IN NO MAN'S LAND

ABOUT THE CAREER OF

Knut Utstein Kloster FATHER OF THE
$20-BILLION-A-YEAR
MODERN CRUISE
INDUSTRY

STEPHANIE GALLAGHER

FOREWORD BY JAMES LOVELOCK

iUniverse books may be ordered through booksellers or by contacting:

iUniverse
1663 Liberty Drive
Bloomington, IN 47403
www.iuniverse.com
1-800-Authors (1-800-288-4677)

Because of the dynamic nature of the Internet, any Web addresses or links contained in this book may have changed since publication and may no longer be valid. The views expressed in this work are solely those of the author and do not necessarily reflect the views of the publisher, and the publisher hereby disclaims any responsibility for them.

ISBN: 978-1-4401-7917-4 (sc)
ISBN: 978-1-4401-7918-1 (hc)
ISBN: 978-1-4401-7916-7 (ebook)

Library of Congress Control Number: 2009937470

Printed in the United States of America

iUniverse rev. date: 09/21/2009

For

My loving husband, Charles Gallagher

In fondest memory of our dearest friend and colleague,
John S. Rogers

With deepest gratitude to and affection
for the late Admiral J. William Kime (U.S.C.G.)
and
"Onwards, Upwards, Excelsior" to the creative brilliance of
Naval Architect Tage Wandborg

CONTENTS

FOREWORD

By James Lovelock

O ver the last forty-four years, I have developed a scientific theory known as Gaia — named after the Greek goddess of Earth. It was the Nobel Laureate novelist, William Golding, who suggested the name Gaia. Under the Gaian theory, all life on Earth and all material parts of the Earth's surface — the air, the oceans, the rocks, and all living organisms — evolved together as a single, inseparable self-regulating system, a living planet. This "living Earth" is able to regulate its climate and composition so as always to be comfortable for the organisms that inhabit it. The Gaia Theory forces a planetary perspective in which humankind is merely part of the whole. It is the health of the planet that matters, not some individual species of organisms. The health of the Earth is now threatened by major changes in natural ecosystems, and we know that humankind bears responsibility for some of this damage. Agriculture and forestry, for example, are seen as serious sources of this kind of damage with the inexorable increase in greenhouse gases, carbon dioxide and methane. Many believe that human activity is associated with, even responsible for, global heating.

Stephanie Gallagher's sensitive and beautifully composed book tells the life story of a remarkable and honourable man, Knut Utstein Kloster. His farsighted vision of a better world and a life spent working to make it possible puts us all in his debt. Kloster touched my life by his unstinted support for Gaia. He also sponsored an important environmental mission in 1991-1992 by sending a replica Viking ship named *GAIA* across the oceans and to the Earth Summit in Rio, gathering messages from the world's children along the vessel's 15,000 mile journey (Chapter Six). I was present in Port Canaveral with Astronaut Jim Lovell to bid *GAIA* a safe passage to Rio.

Kloster is more optimistic than I am. In my most recent book (2009), *The Vanishing Face of Gaia: A Final Warning*, I argue that human beings have already triggered an imminent and unavoidable rapid warming of the planet to the point that it will be able to support fewer of us. So, even though he didn't plan it that way, Kloster's concept of "world cities" at sea holds special appeal; I see them as future lifeboats for a civilization that, hopefully, will learn to live *with* — as opposed to *against* — Mother Nature. I see them as self-sustaining communities that farm the ocean for their needs and in a way that does not threaten the Earth, unlike our land-based civilization.

Kloster's floating cities (Chapters Four and Five) are meant to combine pleasure and purpose, capitalism with a conscience, profit-making with social and environmental responsibility, and based on what I know of this man, he will succeed and I applaud the initiative, in particular the ultimate goal of creating clean, green, environmentally benign global villages (Chapter Nine).

With nearly three quarters of the Earth covered by ocean and with rising sea levels, climate refugees are already flooding into *real* lifeboats — islands and peninsulas which may soon be overcrowded beyond endurance. So whether you believe, as Kloster does, that there is still hope for life as we know it here on Earth, or believe as I do that more and more lifeboats will be needed, it's a perfect time to realize Kloster's vision of ships that are cities at sea — worlds unto themselves, self-sustaining human-scale communities that accept Gaia's rules, rather than waging war against them.

James Lovelock is an independent scientist, inventor, and author of several books, including *The Vanishing Face of Gaia: A Final Warning* (2009), *The Revenge of Gaia* (2006), *Homage to Gaia* (2000), *Gaia: The Practical Science of Planetary Medicine* (1991), *The Ages of Gaia* (1988), and *Gaia, A New Look at Life on Earth* (1979). He has been an Honorary Visiting Fellow of Green Templeton College, University of Oxford since 1994 and the recipient of many honors and awards, and was made a Companion of Honour in 2002 by Her Majesty the Queen (United Kingdom).

ACKNOWLEDGMENTS

First I would like to acknowledge the kind cooperation of my subject, Knut Utstein Kloster. As I note in the Preface, it has been difficult for him to be in the limelight, to have the cameras focused on him, to be praised. But I do praise him. I praise his work, his career, his kindness, his caring, his commitment and, mostly, his example.

In writing this book, I sometimes asked Knut's beautiful, smart, wise and wonderful wife, Trine Kloster, what was her opinion, and whether I had captured the true sense of the man in some sections. Trine, a psychologist, always made helpful observations. I salute her as I salute him.

Many of the activities described in this book were the product of a team effort. I acknowledge with great affection and admiration the hard work and dedication of Knut's principal partners, Tage Wandborg, John S. Rogers, Admiral J. William Kime, Richard Baumler and many others.

Without the love, understanding, patience and sacrifice of Tage Wandborg's wife, Ingrid, he never would have been able to do all that he did — literally design the ships of the future. The spouses of all mentioned, and those included by general reference ("many others"), were equally admirable in their support. I have become very fond of Admiral Kime's wife, Valerie, and Richard Baumler's wife, Joan. Behind every great woman…

I thank my husband, Charles, for his patience and proofreading, as well as his many constructive suggestions as to the content and tone of the book. Same for Tage Wandborg and Richard Baumler. Special thanks to Liv Myhre for her Norwegian-to-English translation of some of the articles and speeches used in the book, for her valued editorial comments, and insight into Norway's Jante Law (see Preface).

Chapters Four and Five — relating to the revolutionary Phoenix World City project and the American Flagship project — are stories unto themselves. That's my next book; but the hundreds of people who have supported the Build America initiative with their creativity, money, time and talent are acknowledged here, in advance of that sequel!

Barbara Colasuonno, Creative Director of Group 33 Design Associates, Inc. in New York, has once again proven her graphic design skills and considerable talents as an editor and proofreader in helping to bring True North to fruition. I thank her not only for her dedication to this project but also for being a joy to work with and a great partner in bringing it all together, cover to cover.

PREFACE

In Norway, they have something called the Jante Law: "Du skal ikke tro at du *er* noe." Freely translated, it means "Don't think that you *are* anything."

The "law" derives from a novel by a Norwegian/Danish author, Aksel Sandemose. The book takes place in an imaginary Danish small town called Jante and describes what the author sees as the unspoken rules of such communities in general. Jante law conveys an important element of Norwegian culture: humility. It teaches people to be modest and to try and see all people as being on equal footing. Norwegians, at least historically, do not flaunt their wealth or financial achievements and look askance at those who do.

Essentially, the main tenets of Jante Law are:

- You shall not think you are special.
- You shall not believe you are smarter than others.
- You shall not believe you are wiser than others.
- You shall not behave as if you are better than others.
- You shall not believe that you know more than others.
- You shall not believe that you can fix things better than others.
- You shall not believe that you can teach others anything.

Norwegians have an egalitarian outlook; they generally express themselves in very modest terms when it comes to compliments and praises. They like people for themselves and not for what they do for a living or for how much money they earn. While this collectivist tradition is gradually giving way to more individualistic values, the concept of Jante Law is still strong in Norway today. Any form of elitism is likely to be met with criticism.

Having explained that characteristic of Norwegian society and culture, the author acknowledges that her Norwegian subject, Knut Utstein Kloster, has been very uncomfortable with this process. He is embarrassed by the attention on himself; he does not think he is special; he does not think he is smarter, wiser, or better than others; he doesn't think he knows more than others or that he can fix things better than others — but I do — and that is why I have chosen to write this story. I think Knut's life, career, concerns and motivations offer an inspiration, a focus on the possible, and an example to be followed.

Knut answered my questions, shared some stories, and provided some of the photographs in this book; but he's not happy to be its subject. He's Norwegian, head to toe, in and out. He thinks he can't teach anybody anything. I think my readers will disagree.

INTRODUCTION

Above all, unto thine own self be true and it shall follow as the day the night, thou can'st not then be false to any man.
Shakespeare — *Hamlet*

Our story is about a visionary man with an impressive career spanning five decades: Knut Utstein Kloster.

Knut is a Norwegian, generally considered the father or founder of the modern cruise industry — an industry which today generates over $20 billion in annual revenues. He is a man of conscience, with a world view. He once described himself as a "flickering soul" in no man's land — the place where his world is secure and comfortable, but where, just beyond reach and in full sight, over 4 billion people live in abject poverty, suffering from preventable diseases and subsisting without basic necessities, most without even electricity.

Globalization and the information age have combined to make the world a very small place where it is more difficult to blur the misery of others or to any longer pretend there is nothing we can do

1

about it. Industrialization of the rich and developed countries has unwittingly contributed enormously to the degradation of the planet, and now our bad example is being replicated by aspiring developing nations and their exploding populations. Knut has never been able to put these realities out of his mind or to conduct his life or operate his business ventures as if they were disconnected from what is happening to the planet and billions of its less fortunate inhabitants. More of us need to feel that connection if civilization, as we know it, is to be sustained.

Knut was Chairman of Klosters Rederi A/S which operated a fleet of cargo ships; he developed an innovative plan for port decongestion that unblocked one of the busiest ports in the world in the 70's and provided a prototype for other developing nations; he founded Norwegian Caribbean Lines (NCL), later renamed Norwegian Cruise Line. Klosters Rederi A/S also owned, for a period, Royal Viking Line and Royal Cruise Line.

Knut played an important role in the 1994 Winter Olympics at Lillehammer, Norway, by developing a traditional Norwegian village, with sod-roofed cottages in designs dating back over the centuries, to house the international media covering the event. The village also contained a large community center which served as the media's headquarters during the games. The government of Norway had insisted that every aspect of the planning for the Olympics conform to the highest possible environmental standards and that all development projects would have a useful life after the games. Today, that mountain village is enjoyed year round by Norwegian families and tourists and is a great asset for the region.

Kloster sponsored a 15,000 mile journey of a replica Viking ship, named *GAIA* after Mother Earth, which gathered thousands of messages of children along her route and delivered them to world leaders in Rio for the 1992 Earth Summit/Global Forum.

This is not a biography but rather career highlights. Much of the story takes place around Kloster's $1.5 billion "city-ship" project, initially known as the "Phoenix project." The Phoenix project spotlights Knut's vision, pioneering spirit, willingness to take risks, and perseverance in the face of seemingly insurmountable obstacles. It also epitomizes the ideal that businesses can have a heart and make a difference and that financial and larger goals can complement one another.

What is particularly exciting about the Phoenix project is its scale and innovation. Although the ship is not yet contracted, the correctness of Knut's vision has already been proven out in the cruise industry. He was *right* when everyone said he was *wrong*, it was *possible* when everyone said it *wasn't*, and decades after he correctly projected where the industry was heading, and how powerfully it would contribute to the international leisure travel business, the project is poised for realization. When the prototype ship is built, it will be all that Knut envisioned it to be, not only an outstanding financial success, but, most importantly, a model of 21st century capitalism.

Whether we call it, as Bill Gates does, "creative capitalism," or as Whole Foods' founder John Mackey does, "conscious capitalism," the new bottom line for 21st century capitalism will measure success based on the company's impact on *all* stakeholders, including the environment and the global community at large.

With marine pollution playing a significant role in the destruction of our environment and ocean ecosystem, Knut has launched a Green Clean Global Village® initiative which will promote green technologies for ships including, where appropriate, advanced atomic engines which will ultimately enable ships to be operated profitably — with zero emissions — in harmony with nature.

Kloster's vision for the ships of the future includes insuring that they operate with minimum impact on the environment.

Throughout his interesting career and challenging business ventures, he has proven the axiom that businesses can "do well by doing good."

Long before green became more than a color, or capitalism came generally to mean more than just profit-making, Knut was investing in socially responsible enterprises that valued all of its stakeholders. The now popular expression, "triple bottom line," was Knut's *modus operandi* from day one. He actively supported the earliest initiatives aimed at improving the environment and promoting the concepts of sustainable development, such as the *Centre for our Common Future*, which took up, on a private level, the excellent work of The World Commission on Environment and Development which had been headed up by former Norwegian Prime Minister, Hon. Gro Harlem Brundtland.

This book highlights some of Knut Utstein Kloster's major business ventures in which he strove to combine financial and larger goals: "2 + 2 = 5," he said, and the formula has guided most of his business decisions from an early age. The story emphasizes the important role of the conscience in navigating a just and equitable course forward. Kloster's "no man's land" is the distance between the world-*that-is* and the world-*as-it-should be*.

You don't have to know or care anything at all about shipping or about the cruise business to enjoy and be inspired by this story. Knut happened to descend from an old and respected shipping family in Norway, so it follows (particularly after the early death of his father) that he stayed in the family business and, as a highly intelligent, restless and adventuresome young man, set out to build on his experience and expand the business in new and exciting directions.

To be touched by this man's life and example, it could have been any other business, but it actually helps the story that Knut is in shipping because of its international character. It is a business in which the stakes are often high, the risks can be immense, and the potential for change and innovation is wide open. Since the oceans represent 70% of the Earth's surface and are, like the skies above, imperiled by pollution and other human activity, Knut's leadership in this area is especially important.

The story about the creation and development of the modern day cruise industry has actually been told very well by Kristoffer A. Garin in his 2005 book, *Devils on the Deep Blue Sea*. Knut wasn't, by the way, one of the "devils" in Garin's book; indeed, he was one of the few angels. But Garin's vivid and historically accurate tale about what has become the fastest growing sector of the leisure travel industry confirms the point that, as an industry, the cruise business provides an exciting backdrop for the story to be told in these pages and for formulating solutions to many of our planet's problems.

Years ago, Knut was given the nickname "True North" because it best described his "true to self/true to values" character and life qualities. No question, this is a man who seems to be guided by a brighter star, pulled by some magnetic force to caring, and driven by an honesty of purpose that all too frequently eludes many of the rest of us in our busy preoccupied daily lives. Thus, his story is inspiring and encouraging. Guided by his internal compass, Knut dares to navigate uncharted waters, to set his sights on the possible. His business ventures are exciting and demonstrate that entrepreneurialism and larger goals can go hand-in-hand and benefit one another.

CHAPTER ONE
Seeing the Future — and Going For It

S ome people are born visionaries — they see the future, both its
prospects and its potential problems. Seeing the future enables one
to take action, to take risks, and to make decisions which capitalize
on the prospects and, with some planning and luck, hopefully steer
clear of the problems.

Knut Utstein Kloster is such a visionary, not only about the
prospects and potential pitfalls of his business ventures, but also in
the larger sense, in terms of the human condition and the state of
the world.

"Set your course by distant stars, not by the light of passing
ships." This is one of his favorite sayings. And that is what he has
done his whole life.

Knut was barely 30 years of age when his father died and he
therefore took the helm of the family shipping business in Oslo.
He had been educated in the United States at the Massachusetts
Institute of Technology (MIT) in naval architecture and marine
engineering.

In 1964, questioning the need for diversification of his

company's cargo fleet, Knut commissioned an advanced, specially-designed passenger-and-car liner. The plan was to engage the ship in weekly service between Southampton and Gibraltar, with calls at Vigo, Spain and Lisbon, Portugal. Tourists could take their cars on the ship or have the option of driving down and cruising back on a seven-day round trip schedule.

This is a good time to introduce Knut's closest collaborator, Tage Wandborg, likely the world's greatest and surely its most prolific naval architect. A Dane, Tage was entrusted to convert Kloster's vision into steel. At that time, Tage was working as Chief Designer in a Copenhagen-based consulting naval architecture firm. He was an innovator and trendsetter in the construction of passenger-and-car liners all over the world.

The first 'cruise' ship

Tage Wandborg was asked by Kloster to design a large, purpose-built passenger-and-car liner that could provide a safe and comfortable ride for passengers en route to the Mediterranean via the often-stormy waters of the Bay of Biscay.

The result was a highly advanced, efficient and futuristic yacht-style liner which was to pioneer the modern cruise industry. The ship was built in Norway and named *M/S SUNWARD*.

The operation of *M/S SUNWARD* started in 1966 and was a great success, *at first.* Then two things happened which changed the economic prospects of the enterprise dramatically. The United Kingdom enacted a law that restricted the currency which U.K. citizens could take out of the country, and Spain's General Franco closed the frontier between Spain and Gibraltar, meaning the U.K. tourists couldn't get past the border into Spain.

NCL's M/S SUNWARD was an ultra modern, highly efficient, yacht-style passenger-and-car liner.

Meanwhile, in Miami, Ted Arison (who later founded Carnival Cruise Lines) was marketing two Israeli-owned car ferries on short cruises to the Bahamas. The sudden bankruptcy of the Israeli shipowners and arrest of their ships by creditors had left Arison with booked passengers but no ships.

At this point, Arison learned of the fate of Kloster's U.K.-to-Spain passenger-and-car ferry service and of the possible availability of the ultra-modern *M/S SUNWARD*. Arison contacted Kloster who made a quick decision to transfer the ship to Miami and engage her in three and four day cruises to the Bahamas.

Always with foresight, Kloster had ordered a ship with air conditioning capacity, in case she would ultimately serve in warmer climates. Every cabin had private facilities which were quite unusual for passenger-and-car ferries at that time. Ted Arison became the agent of Klosters Rederi A/S. A new company was formed, Norwegian Caribbean Lines (NCL), to operate the ship.

Here we see the pioneering M/S SUNWARD in Southampton, summer 1966, in the company of some of Britain's most famous liners.

M/S SUNWARD sailed a few weeks later from Miami on a 1966 Christmas cruise. The operation of the ship in the Caribbean trade was an immediate success.

Off and running: M/S STARWARD and M/S SKYWARD

Six months later, Kloster asked Tage Wandborg to design the optimum cruise ship for this new market. However, Knut indicated that he still wanted the new ships to have some roll-on/roll-off freight capacity, in case of a change in the demand for cruises. Orders were placed with a German shipyard in Bremerhaven, and the ships were later christened *M/S STARWARD* and *M/S SKYWARD*.

The new ships were to be 12,940 GRT[1] with a capacity for 540 passengers and 220 cars or other vehicles. Halfway into the building

---

[1] GRT means gross registered tons, a cubic (not weight) measurement.

period, with the demand for cruises on *M/S SUNWARD* greatly exceeding capacity, Knut asked Tage if he could change the design, mid-construction, to exclude the freight capacity and to add more passenger capacity. Tage arranged a meeting with the shipyard and presented his design suggestions for eliminating the freight capacity and adding more guest cabins. The yard accepted the proposal and the first purpose-built cruise ship (delivered on time and on budget) was successfully introduced into the Caribbean market.

Full speed ahead: M/S SOUTHWARD and M/S SEAWARD

Success breeds success and two sister ships of *M/S STARWARD* and *M/S SKYWARD* were ordered by Kloster from an Italian shipyard. When Tage learned of Knut's order for the newbuilds, he informed Knut that there was an opportunity to introduce still further design innovations which would make the ships even more appealing and appropriate for the cruise market. Knut and Tage traveled to Italy to see if the yard could be persuaded to alter the contract design in accordance with Tage's further design innovations. The yard recognized that it would enhance their own reputation to introduce such future-oriented cruise ships and the plan was accepted without a change in budget. The two new ships were to be named *M/S SOUTHWARD* and *M/S SEAWARD*.

Then the glitch — but honor above all

Shortly before the two new ships were to be delivered by the state-owned Italian shipyard, Kloster received a disturbing message from the shipyard that both contracts had been cancelled. The contract for each ship had been $13 million and advance bookings had already been made for both ships. The yard referred to some statutory provision from the Mussolini era which permitted a state-owned facility to cancel a contract that resulted in the state losing money. Lawyers were dispatched to Italy. In a private meeting with a government official, NCL's lawyers were told that one million dollars to a numbered Swiss bank account would resolve the matter. There is probably no need to tell my readers, even this early on in the story, that Knut was not about to wire money into a Swiss bank account. "It was morally and legally impossible," he said.

After lengthy negotiations, the *M/S SOUTHWARD* was delivered on budget, but the second ship, *M/S SEAWARD*, was, instead, sold for $20 million to P & O, and became the *SPIRIT OF LONDON* — a costly setback for NCL. For Knut, it was a matter of conscience, "a shabby affair, but forget it and move on."

First fleet of the Caribbean

With the delivery of *M/S SOUTHWARD*, Kloster had four ships delivered within four years — and the modern cruise industry was born.

Growth continues: SUNWARD II

In 1973, Knut decided to sell the passenger-and-car ferry, *M/S SUNWARD*, and to acquire a vessel with additional passenger capacity to meet ever-increasing demand. It was learned that the *CUNARD ADVENTURE* was for sale. Coincidentally, Tage Wandborg had designed this ship for another client, but when Cunard acquired it, a different naval architect was retained to change the exterior of the ship so that it would replicate the sheer lines of Cunard's *QE II*.

Knut asked Tage to redesign the ship so that it would match the futuristic yacht-style of the other NCL ships, now known as the "white fleet." After the conversion, the ship was christened *M/S SUNWARD II.*

"Kloster – A Modern Shipowner"

In 1971, when Knut was visiting Genoa for the sea trials of the *M/S SOUTHWARD*, reporters from the local newspaper, *Ritratti*, interviewed him. The headline of the article was "Kloster – A Modern Shipowner." Of course, there was no mention in the article about the cancellation of the contract for of the *M/S SEAWARD*. But the *Ritratti* article (roughly translated) captures the essence of the man:

> Talking with the reporters on board, he [Kloster] has made some comments about the working conditions in the Italian factories.
>
> "The workers are not treated well," he said. "I don't mean economically, they can earn good money, but they don't feel respected in the factory…the workers must only obey orders without any possibility of telling their opinions…"
>
> Who is this Norwegian gentleman? He cannot be similarly compared to our own shipowners.
>
> His name is Knut, a navigator's name, he is 42 years old, about 1 meter and 90 centimeters tall, handsome and athletically perfect. He is the third generation of the Kloster family of Oslo, a family that has owned ships since 1905. He is an intelligent man with quick answers…He works seriously at his profession. He is a naval architect, which he studied to be at the Massachusetts Institute of Technology in Boston in the United States. Courteous and precise, he answers all questions without difficulty. But as soon as the opportunity comes, he is quick to ask the questions.
>
> "You want to know me? Good. I want to know you, too. Let's talk about things that interest us both."
>
> We spoke about books. This Norwegian shipowner reads methodically every day, not only those books that are of interest to his profession. Flying from Miami, he spent his time reading *The*

Revue of the Merchant Marine, regarding ships, and *The Greening of America*, an historical-sociological book written by a Yale professor. It is not the first time he read this book. "This is a really marvelous book. It gave me an answer to a question that I have been thinking about for a long time. I have asked myself many times — Where is the society going? Charles Reich, the author, speaks of the United States, but in discussing the book it looks like he could be speaking about the old Europe as well."

Kloster says that from reading the book he can understand what a serious condition all societies are in. To change that condition we have to change our attitude toward money, our fellow human beings and life in general. Knut Utstein Kloster is not a pessimist. Rather he is a great optimist and also has the spirit of reformation.

Tracing a pyramid on a piece of paper he showed me a type of organizational structure. "See how far the top is from the base? It is the same thing in many industries. The owner and the executives are on the top and the employees are on the bottom. This cannot go on this way, from a human standpoint and also an economical standpoint. What social benefit has an industry where few give orders and everyone else has to obey them? The direction has to be very firm from the top, certainly, but then we have to squash the pyramid so that the distance between the top and the base is diminished so that employees can have more responsibility."

Is this a product of fantasy or vision? "Maybe," Kloster said. "But something is certain; things have to change and be done in a new way or else it will be bad for Americans, Europeans and everyone else."

He knows he is criticized. In Norway, some consider him a dangerous socialist, others a terrible capitalist. In the meantime, somebody else compares him to Joan of Arc, the Saint of Orleans. "Yes, Yes, Yes," Kloster commented, smiling, but not happy with it…

Before the interviewer left, Kloster asked him very seriously, "Do you think we are doing something good, taking people on cruises?"

The question has haunted Knut for many years.

Rx for Tourism's 'Cultural Disparity'

A year before that interview in Genoa, *The New York Times* then travel editor, Paul J.C. Friedlander, wrote an article (December 6, 1970) entitled "Rx for Tourism's 'Cultural Disparity.' " The article described an early effort on the part of Kloster and NCL to close the gap between tourists and peoples and cultures they visit. Friedlander defined "cultural disparity" as "what happens when an affluent tourist who steps off a big airplane or luxury cruise liner, looks at the local shopkeeper, the waiter or chauffeur but doesn't really see him; when he talks at the locals he happens to brush against in some commercial context but never communicates or really talks *with* them. The disorientation works equally the other way when the local sees the visitor as a parasite to be fleeced or given as fast a back of the hand as possible — or, in extremes, as an evil not completely necessary."

The New York Times article is about the "New Experiences" program which Kloster instituted in 1970 for passengers sailing on NCL's *M/S STARWARD* from Miami to Jamaica. The basic idea behind the "New Experiences" program was to help interested passengers learn something about the island countries they were about to visit and to have genuine exchanges with local residents when they reached the island destination. To quote *The New York Times* article:

> The way the "New Experiences" program came about is as
> interesting as the program's potentialities. It started…as
> a directive from Oslo's Knut Utstein Kloster,… who owns,
> along with a large Oslo-based fleet, the *M/S Starward* and
> her two sisters, the *M/S Sunward* and the *M/S Skyward*, and

Norwegian Caribbean Lines. Kloster's directive raised the question of what the cruise line was doing for its passengers and for its destination countries. He had observed the cultural disparity that diminished what many passengers get out of their cruises, and he warned that unless something was done to bridge this obvious gap there might come a time when American tourists would not want to go to those destinations, and when the locals and their governments might no longer welcome such visitors.

Kloster's challenge, as Friedlander observed, was "idealistic but also practical" because cruise lines must have destinations where their passengers are welcome. The ultimate goal of the program was to create the foundation for a positive attitude toward cruise passengers among the populations of the various islands visited and to enrich the experience for passengers.

In an interview with *Cruise Industry News* in 1999, "Knut Utstein Kloster – A Man of Vision", Knut explains his "idealistic but also practical" philosophy:

> In my book, being profitable means getting a good return on capital, defined as money, human resources and influence. The money side is obvious. You cannot talk about being profitable unless there is a healthy bottom line. But you also have the human resources side with all the people employed by the company. The return on this capital, broadly speaking, is reflected in the level of employee satisfaction and job performance. And then there is the influence side. By that I mean the company's potential for creating an environment in which it and the free enterprise concept will thrive — simply because people feel good about it.

The Shape of Things to Come

In 1972, Knut delivered a speech at the Convention of the Association of British Travel Agents, held in Vienna. The theme of the conference was "The Shape of Things to Come." In his speech, he got quickly to the point:

> I could stand here today and describe for you in detail the physical shape of our future ships as I would envisage them… There would seem to be a certain degree of excitement in that, as the key to leadership in today's cruise industry is largely based on one's ability to maintain the newest, most modern fleet.
>
> But I am not going to dwell much on that, because I don't believe that Newness itself will be the keynote of leadership in the future. I am convinced that our ability to meet the challenge of tomorrow will depend not so much on the physical shape of the ships, as on what we put into them…
>
> As I see it, the business of tourism, as all business, will ultimately have to be responsible to the society and ecology in which it exists.

This, of course, echoes the current mantra of corporate citizenship, where increasingly, corporations are interpreting the "bottom line" not only as their profit, but also, the manner in which employees are treated, and the impact of their businesses on the community and on the environment. All stakeholders must be included. Knut saw this from the very beginning of his career.

Trouble in Paradise

Despite the tremendous success of the new NCL venture in Miami, Knut's relationship with Ted Arison disintegrated when it was learned that Arison had been diverting, for his personal use, the passengers' prepaid cruise fares. Arison claimed that the money didn't belong to NCL until after the cruise had been concluded, but the contract he had signed with Klosters Rederi A/S expressly provided that all revenues were to be deposited into the Klosters Rederi account within 24 hours. That didn't happen.

The agency relationship between Arison and NCL ended and litigation ensued. It was a sad day for Knut; he had been close to Ted, his wife Lin, his son Mickey — and Ted's genius had most certainly contributed greatly to the success of the business. According to Knut, and as detailed in Kristoffer Garin's book, *Devils on the Deep Blue Sea*, after the breakup, Arison withheld NCL's passenger lists and millions of dollars in prepaid cruise fares. Ted used the monies to start his own company, Carnival Cruise Lines. Carnival grew to be the giant in the industry.

Although the enormously successful Arison later became well known for his community generosity and civic-mindedness, amends were never made with Knut or NCL. Ted Arison died in 2005. His son, Mickey, now runs the company. It's never too late to set things right.

CHAPTER TWO
On the Other Side of the Globe...

In some countries throughout the world in the early 70's, port congestion was a serious impediment to development. With virtual armadas of cargo ships lying at anchor outside clogged ports, vital materials — machinery, goods, foodstuffs and equipment of every type — were effectively blocked from entering these countries, seriously impeding the growth and development within those nations.

This was the situation in Saudi Arabia in the boom days of that nation's oil-spurred development. There was a great need for materials which were being shipped from all over the world, but, because of inadequately built port facilities, the ships could not dock to unload their cargos. There were, for example, at the Port of Jeddah, queues of up to 90 ships which had to wait, often in excess of 100 days, to discharge cargoes. The result was a huge waste of resources, crew time and ship service, resulting in higher costs for transported goods, rapid inflation and a ripple effect that touched many other national economies. In a public statement made at the time, Knut said:

> Our firm has been turning its attention to the problems which
> different developing countries have in the disembarkment
> of cargoes. We found that large development projects have

become paralyzed because building materials and equipment are not getting to their destination. Port operations in many places are bottlenecked by narrow streets and poor quality landing equipment in seaport towns. Although in most such countries the authorities make wholehearted efforts to find solutions to these problems, traffic in seaport towns has increased to the point where it exceeds the authorities' ability to cope. We decided to make contact with authorities in Saudi Arabia, and, after a period of planning, set up our project in Jeddah.

Kloster saw the port congestion problem as a "pilot project of poetic simplicity." He purchased five laid-up U.S. Navy LSTs (Landing Ship Tank) originally designed and built for the United States Navy during World War II to serve as ocean-going, amphibious ships for transporting and landing troops and tanks on invasion beachheads. The idea was to unload the cargo from ships at their anchorage, store the cargo onboard the LSTs in semi-trailers which are then unloaded (landed) on the beach where the cargo is then transported in the semi-trailers to various inland destinations, bypassing the crowded port. From ship at anchorage to destination, the cargo is handled once, in the sense that the stowed medium (the semi-trailers) remain with their load throughout the entire operation and until delivery.

Working with Resources and Industries Associates Group (RIA) — a multi-country endeavor organized to pool talents and resources to benefit developing nations — Kloster arranged for conversion of the five LSTs. The main feature of the conversion was the installation of long drop-ramps from the upper to the lower deck. The existing ramps, intended for running tanks between decks, were not suitable for the semi-trailers to be used in this application. Each ship was to take approximately 50 semi-trailers onboard using both the upper and lower deck. The cargo would be loaded directly on to

these semi-trailers which, in turn, would be trucked ashore through the ship's original bow door and landing ramp arrangement. Another aspect of the conversion was to reinforce the upper decks with wood planking in order to provide a smooth surface for the trailers and redistribute their weight. Amazingly, the conversion of all five ships

was accomplished in only two months time.

Klosters Rederi A/S joined with a Saudi company to take charge of the harbor operations. The company was called Land-Sea Transport Company (LSTCO). Kloster's part of the operation involved unloading the cargo and getting it to the shore where a South Korean company took over for the land transport of the cargo. Knut chartered a passenger ship to accommodate the ships' officers and crew of over 1,200. His investment was $20 million. After only a few months, the LSTs had disembarked over 500,000 tons of cargo which was a very high percentage of all the total goods landing at Jeddah. The operation had the direct result of reducing the cost of consumer goods, flattening the inflation curve in that country, and serving as a prototype for solving port congestion problems in other developing countries.

Another byproduct of this successful turnkey prototype project was Knut's relationship with New York admiralty counsel, John S. Rogers, who helped coordinate the LSTCO project with Saudi authorities and who would later become Knut's partner in several other challenging ventures described in this book.

CHAPTER THREE
Make No Little Plans

"See first that the design is wise and just; that ascertained, pursue it resolutely."
— Shakespeare

In everything he does, Knut thinks outside the box. He thinks big and aims high. If he believes in something — if he sets his sights on accomplishing something — he will pursue it resolutely and not be deterred by the skepticism of others, nor by setbacks or delays. He is a man of strong convictions, with the courage to follow both his head — and his heart.

The cruise business in Miami took off like wildfire. Knut's vision spurred competition and before long, there were several cruise companies competing for what appeared to be — and has proven to be — an endless supply of cruise passengers.

Each new ship brought on line was a somewhat larger version of its predecessor, but there were no significant innovations, size or otherwise, and the largest ships accommodated only about 700-800 passengers.

After his disappointing breakup with Ted Arison in 1971, Knut continued at the helm of NCL. He had four very successful ships in operation but it became clear as the light of day to him that the industry was not meeting the rising expectations of cruise passengers or capturing its full potential as an industry.

Land-based resorts offered many more options and amenities. Knut envisioned a floating resort that could compete with — and surpass — his land-based competition, adding the important element of a journey at sea. His cruise company rivals, on the other hand, proceeded with cautious optimism, choosing to expand and grow very gradually. The problem with building newer, bigger, better ships is that, in a sense, they undermine the existing fleet whose profits are needed to fund the new construction.

Kloster, always a maverick, was restless to break the mold. With his brilliant collaborator, naval architect Tage Wandborg, he considered all options — building a new ship or perhaps converting one of the great transatlantic ocean liners of the past. Many of these great ships had been laid up with the onslaught of air travel. Knut's ultimate choice, the *S/S FRANCE*, was viewed by rival cruise lines with utter disbelief; they saw it as "suicide" and didn't miss an opportunity to share their views and skepticism with the media.

The *S/S FRANCE* had been built in 1957 at a time when the era of transatlantic crossings was already losing ground to the air travel industry. By 1960, when the *S/S FRANCE* was launched, jet travel had taken over 70% of transatlantic travel. In 1962, after a five year construction period, during which time no expense had been spared, the *S/S FRANCE* made her maiden voyage to New York. It is reported that, by the end of the decade, few travelers, less than 4%, preferred a five-day sea voyage to a six hour flight. With the first oil crisis, it was clear that the *S/S FRANCE* could not survive economically and, after only twelve years in service, she was laid up. The golden age of transatlantic liners was over.

When Tage Wandborg first visited the *S/S FRANCE* in 1979 at Knut's request, she was laying alongside the appropriately named "Quay of Oblivion." Tage was taken aback by her beauty and majesty. "She was a masterpiece of marine engineering," he said. "The materials that went into her construction and engineering were the very best that money could buy. I felt awed by the sheer size of her hull and by her grace and elegance."

Tage spent two days on board the *S/S FRANCE* on that first visit. He returned shortly thereafter to Oslo and reported his observations to Knut who then asked how long it would take for Tage to say yes or no to the possibility of converting this transatlantic liner into a sophisticated cruise ship for the Caribbean. Tage asked for three weeks.

He hurried back to Le Havre, taking with him a team of experts. When the three weeks were up, he returned to Oslo and presented his conversion proposals to Knut and concluded the presentation with a resounding, "Yes, it can be done!"

Knut asked Tage to return to the ship with his team to work out complete documentation and invite shipyards to bid on the conversion. In the meantime, Knut started negotiations for the purchase of the ship. The vessel was acquired by Klosters Rederi A/S, under the NCL banner, and renamed

Knut and his wife, Trine Kloster, visit the S/S FRANCE for the first time.

S/S NORWAY. A German yard was selected for the momentous conversion.

However, when the vessel was ready to leave the port of Le Havre, to be towed to Bremerhaven, the French Workers Union protested vehemently that *S/S FRANCE* — proud symbol of the nation's maritime heritage — should leave the country. Thousands of people blocked the bridge which had to be opened to permit the vessel to be freed from her "Quay of Oblivion," where she has been kept in seclusion for the previous five years. Ultimately, the police were able to clear the bridge and *S/S FRANCE* bid adieu to her homeland. It has been reliably reported to this author that Kloster's fair treatment of his crews, and verification of this to French labor unions, played a role in resolving the difficult controversy.

Having been built for transatlantic crossings, the *S/S FRANCE* was a closed-in vessel to protect the interior from the ravages of the North Atlantic. Tage's job was to open her up to the Caribbean warmth and sunshine. As with the other transatlantic liners of her

Members of the French Workers Union initially tried to block the bridge to prevent the S/S FRANCE from leaving the country.

time, the *S/S FRANCE* was also a two-class ship. Kloster wanted the ship to be a classless ship where all the passengers could associate with one another and move about freely, without barriers. The one-time promenade decks were converted into two main thoroughfares, the Champs-Élysées and Fifth Avenue, which were later to be filled with shops, bars, cafés, restaurants, night clubs, galleries, etc.

When Knut went aboard the *S/S FRANCE* for the first time, he commented that "she seemed to be smiling at us; she seemed to know we had her best interests at heart." Knut had been given a 30 day option to purchase the ship and, within that time, based on Tage's report, he resolved to buy her. The price was $18 million. Even with the approximately $100 million refurbishment costs, it was a bargain and significantly less than the cost of a new ship of comparable size.

The *S/S NORWAY* was more than triple the size of any other ship serving the Caribbean cruise market. She was 66,000 tons, 1,035 feet (six city blocks) and accommodated 2,400 passengers. Instantly, it was the world's largest cruise ship and she held that record for over a decade.

Kloster's decision changed the industry overnight. The *S/S NORWAY* heralded a new generation of cruise ships that sought to combine many of the amenities of land-based resorts with the enchantment of a sea voyage. It was an entirely new and very exciting hospitality product. In addition to the traditional main dining rooms, the *S/S NORWAY* offered multiple restaurants, cafés, bars, lounges and a disco. The ship's huge theatre, which could accommodate 500 guests, soared three decks high and offered full-scale Broadway productions. Compared to conventional cruising, there were seemingly boundless opportunities for sport and fitness, shopping, recreation and entertainment.

The *S/S NORWAY* represented 40% of the total passenger capacity sailing year-round in the Caribbean. For all their skepticism at the announcement of the acquisition, the industry scurried to catch up.

In 1984, a tribute in words and pictures was published about the *S/S NORWAY*, still, at that time, the world's largest ship. Norwegian journalist, Alf G. Andersen, who contributed to the publication, had this to say about Knut:

> A lot of people are surprised that Kloster has not adopted the trappings and opinions commonly associated with the shipowning elite. He openly sympathizes with ideas and movements that spring from society's grassroots, so much so that in some quarters he is suspect for holding too controversial views. "I don't feel like a revolutionary," Kloster said. "I just follow my own guiding star, and it's up to other people to follow theirs. We all seek to do what we consider to be right and proper. I don't think stereotyped thinking should be allowed to replace an independent viewpoint and initiative."

> Knut Utstein Kloster's Norwegian Caribbean Lines have built up a cruise empire. People from the world's industrial nations board the company's ships and are carried in comfort

to countries and places where hunger is a fact of life. The company earns its livelihood in the border zone between affluence and abject poverty.

"Don't you find the contrast disquieting?" Mr. Andersen asked of Knut.

His answer: "I've never disguised the fact that I'm concerned with the impact of the cruise trade on Third World countries. I'm sure that it may safely be said that tourism helps to promote economic development, international understanding and community feeling. And there's no doubt that our cruises mean a great deal to the Caribbean countries visited by our ships and from which many of our crew members are recruited. But there's certainly another side to the coin, too. The collision of cultures that cruising involves provides considerable food for thought. And the long-term effects of the development cruising fosters are also open to question. But however one looks at it the fact remains that our cruise activity has generated a vast amount of employment."

The decision to buy and convert the *S/S FRANCE* required vision, courage and conviction. These are the same traits required of today's corporate and community leadership regardless of the nature of the endeavor.

Knut looked at the *S/S NORWAY*, with its diverse nationalities of officers, passengers and crew, as a mini United Nations. There were between 25 and 30 different nations represented at all times in the crew of the ship. Add to that the multi-racial and multi-national backgrounds of the societies visited by the ship during her travels, and it's easy to see that the *S/S NORWAY* was truly a "Little United Nations" afloat. Knut contacted the UN to request permission to fly the UN flag on board the ship. Permission was granted by the (then) Secretary-General, Hon. Kurt Waldheim. The flag was hoisted at a special ceremony in 1981 when the ship visited her home port of Oslo. The ceremony was attended by His Majesty King Olav V of Norway, and Their Royal Highnesses, Crown Prince Harald and Crown Princess Sonja.

Knut's "Little United Nations" is a theme he has advanced for many years in other contexts. Whenever there is an opportunity to demonstrate that we are all in the 'same boat' and share responsibility for steering a just and sustainable course forward, Knut seizes it.

This desire, on Knut's part, to use his ships to bring people together and address problems of common concern, was to become a recurring theme in his life.

CHAPTER FOUR
Come, Let Us Build Us a City

A great city – a great solitude.
English proverb

With the success of the *S/S NORWAY*, Knut and Tage were convinced that the mega-ship concept was the way of the future and that the next leap would be to a size that liberated passenger accommodations from the confinement of the hull, thereby dramatically increasing the cubic space in the hull for other purposes. The result would be an island at sea, with three hotel towers rising boldly into the sunlight and sea air, offering vistas of the ship and the ocean from every guest room, and freeing up space in the hull for all the facilities and amenities which one would expect to find in a resort town or cultural center ashore, and much more! What they envisioned was, quite literally, a city-at-sea.

Knut dubbed the project "Phoenix" — named with the project's larger goals in mind. Phoenix is the ancient symbol of human aspiration toward universal good and of self-renewal.

Although one of the most extensive market surveys that had

ever been commissioned in the travel industry confirmed the viability of the Phoenix concept, some of Knut's fellow executives at NCL disagreed with him, and they argued that a number of new conventional size ships was needed to maintain NCL's share of the market. Moreover, at the time, NCL was preparing to go public and some board members felt that such a revolutionary project in the presentation of the company would be unwise. Too risky. NCL, then the most popular cruise line in the world (thanks mostly to the *S/S NORWAY*), ultimately decided not to pursue the Phoenix project. Knut recalls the decision-making process:

> At a board meeting in Miami, when the company's strategy
> was being discussed, I asked NCL's (then) Senior VP of

Floating city of the future: a 5' x 6' oil painting by the American artist, Robert T. McCall, renowned for his space art and particularly his six-story mural at the National Air & Space Museum of man's historic landing on the moon.

Sales and Marketing what he would go for in a newbuilding program if the choice was between Phoenix and three conventional newbuildings with the same total capacity. He chose Phoenix. When I asked him why, he said, "Because I know I can fill the Phoenix to capacity in the first three years, at least — without any advertising." He expressed confidence that the ship's uniqueness, appeal, even celebrity as the world's largest ship would provide all the promotion needed to fill the ship.

But it wasn't to be. Knut respectfully resigned as Chairman and CEO, gave up his NCL directorship, and bought the Phoenix project from NCL, to be developed by him as a stand-alone venture. One of the qualities that Knut has exhibited throughout his life is the ability to stay the course, to have faith in his convictions and not be deterred by difficulty in pursuing his objectives.

World City Corporation was formed in Oslo and New York to develop the project. Knut and his New York partner, John S. Rogers, whom he had met in Saudi Arabia on the LSTCO port decongestion project (Chapter Two), came up with the name "World City" because it best described what they envisioned for life on board the city-ship and the larger goals to be achieved through its realization. It is borrowed from, among others, the works of Lewis Mumford who wrote extensively about urban civilization. In his seminal work, *The City in History*, Mumford uses the example of the medieval city as the basis for the "ideal city" where the best and most vital human talents and resources are brought together and integrated — the 'cosmopolitan' ideal. This is what Knut and John Rogers envisioned for Phoenix and the city-ship was thereafter known as *PHOENIX WORLD CITY*. Tage Wandborg set about to convert the vision into a design that would shape the future of the industry — in both size and concept.

At the same time, World City Foundation was also established.

Its goals were to promote sustainable development, environmental protection and international understanding, as well as to fund programs and initiatives that foster leadership, citizenship, corporate and social responsibility, business ethics, scientific and technological achievement, global awareness, and educational and cultural enrichment.

The idea was to steer a portion of the profits from the operation of the ship to the foundation to support these larger goals, and to use the ship itself to maximize its unique environment as a cross-cultural forum and global meeting place. The harnessing of this major capital asset for the attainment of shared international goals was part of a growing trend among world business organizations to assume a more active role in creating a healthier society and a more habitable planet.

When the late John J. McCloy[2] learned of Kloster's plans for World City Foundation, he wrote:

> It is an imperative that leaders in all fields make every effort
> to develop constructive interdependence among nations
> and improve the international decision making process. The
> concept of introducing business leaders into the picture at this
> stage in world history is a very great one. What can I do to help?

Saburo Okita, Japan's former Foreign Minister and world-recognized economist and social planner, became a Senior Advisor to the Foundation and wrote:

> This new endeavor has a very real opportunity to contribute
> significantly to the global community by helping to integrate
> national and international needs and interests in every field.

---

[2] John J. McCloy was the Former High Commissioner for Germany; first President of the World Bank; former Chairman of Chase Manhattan Bank; former Chairman of the Ford Foundation; and former Hon. Chairman of the Foreign Relations Council.

World City Foundation was to provide a vehicle — and a process — for activating a sense of world community and encouraging new dimensions of personal growth and development in all human cultures. The late Joseph Elliot Slater[3] became Chairman of the Foundation.

The goals of the Foundation are:

...to maximize *PHOENIX WORLD CITY'S* unique environment as a cross-cultural forum and global meeting place

...to demonstrate, in all of the Foundation's activities, that human potential is the greatest resource on Earth

...to articulate, in as many ways and for as many people as possible, a positive and achievable vision of the future

...to create a climate for the free exchange of ideas, the process of creativity and renewal, and the pursuit of excellence

...to foster and encourage a new generation of leadership and decision making which is more human, more globally-oriented, and responsive to transnational problems and opportunities

[3] Joe Slater brought to the task a broad range of international experience in both the public and private sectors. He had served as Chief Economist of the Creole Petroleum Co., where he founded and directed the Creole Foundation; Program Officer in charge of the International Affairs Program of the Ford Foundation; President of the Salk Institute; and, for almost two decades, President of the Aspen Institute for Humanistic Studies.

…to bring together the best in ideas, talents and institutions to focus on new and more effective ways of looking at, thinking about and responding constructively to global issues and challenges and

…to engage the global business community and world leadership in a socially responsible, transnational mobilization of their productive endeavors…

… for the common good

John S. Rogers, Knut Kloster and Tage Wandborg present the PHOENIX WORLD CITY project.

The late Austrian political scientist and economist, Dr. Leopold Kohr, originator of the "small is beautiful" philosophy, often wrote about the ideal "human scale" community and dedicated a chapter to *PHOENIX WORLD CITY*, "by far the largest ship ever," in his book, *The Inner City*.

> How can I incorporate it in my smallness philosophy? As its name World City indicates, the point is that it is not so much the largest boat as the smallest planet; not the meaningless expanse of the world that includes a city, but a city that is a world in itself, "the universe in a little room," as Marlowe put it or, as Aristotle said in his definition of the ideal size of the state, "one that can be taken in at a single view." There will be no danger of the modern disease of inner city neglect and decay for it will be prevented from spilling over its 'walls' into the ocean, and the inner city as it always used to be will be the entire city once again. Phoenix arisen anew.

Kloster saw an opportunity to take the success, appeal and growth of the cruise industry and create an entirely new product that would attract a much larger segment of the travel and leisure market — and, importantly, contribute to public awareness and participation in issues larger than self. In addition to being a vacation paradise, offering every conceivable opportunity for guests to enjoy, entertain and enrich themselves, *PHOENIX WORLD CITY* also was designed to serve as a global forum for important corporate, educational, cultural and international events and activities, further enhancing its marketability. The objective was to bring together thought leaders in business, government, science, education and public service, and to encourage them to use this congenial and stimulating environment to think creatively about common issues and global challenges.

Leopold Kohr had developed the concept of the Academic Inn© — a convivial place where people could gather and talk about the issues of the times. This concept derives from the tavern which was, with a church and a town hall, the center of the "inner city" activity in ancient human-scale towns and villages. Leopold kindly suggested that an Academic Inn© on board *PHOENIX WORLD CITY* would become an inviting place where visiting scholars, scientists, poets, authors, thought-leaders, professors, etc. could mingle with guests and, through lively conversation and the exchange of ideas, enrich the experience for all. And so it will be.

In an early description of the project, Knut wrote:

> *PHOENIX WORLD CITY* encompasses both a place and an ideal. As place, it will be a unique world-class resort and global forum; as an ideal, it will symbolize the process of international cooperation, understanding and exchange. By creating a network of ideas, people, organizations and institutions, we will enable participants to take positive steps toward resolution of differences, and toward improving the prospects for peace and world order.

The city-ship concept is, of course, less of a technological challenge today than when Knut and Tage first conceived of it. This is because, in the meantime, the modular methodology for building such a large ship has been developed and perfected, and the most challenging technical issues have been addressed and solved, many by World City's own design and engineering team in collaboration with the world's leading technology providers and regulatory agencies including the Norwegian Maritime Directorate, Det Norsk Veritas, the United States Coast Guard and American Bureau of Shipping. The industry has grown, exactly as Knut predicted, and, over time, ships have become larger and larger and many of the innovations developed in the context of the Phoenix project have been emulated by other shipowners in their newbuild projects.

The Phoenix project has already revolutionized the cruise industry and the cruise experience. It was far ahead of its time but dead-on right as the optimum size, design and concept for capturing the full potential of the industry. Almost two decades later, and after an investment of over $55 million, the city-ship will still be the world's largest and most unique vessel. And, unlike its competition, a great deal of investment has gone into the software side of the city-ship; the onboard experience will be like no other place on earth. Also significant is the combination of profit-making with a deeper purpose. Through its operations, the city-ship will support worthwhile initiatives in education, environment and development. When he first learned of the World City project, Maurice Strong, former Under Secretary-General of the United Nations and first Executive Director of the United Nations Environment Programme, wrote:

> There is really nothing quite like it, and I have a strong and growing feeling that the World City project can become a global focal point for the kind of energies and initiatives required to ensure a more secure and hopeful future for the entire human family in the century ahead.

The Hon. Gro Harlem Brundtland, former Prime Minister of Norway and Chairman of the UN World Commission on Environment and Development, praised the initiative as responsive to "the call for action" of the World Commission. She emphasized that "private enterprise has a clear responsibility for the future of the world" and that such future-oriented commitments will "contribute to the widening of perspective which is so urgently needed."

Peter V. Ueberroth, well-known for his superb organization of the 1984 Olympics and as U.S. Baseball Commissioner, is less known for his expertise in the leisure travel business. Peter founded a travel business in 1963 which became the second largest in North America by 1980 when he sold it to the late Curt Carlson, of Carlson Companies, the Minnesota-based hospitality powerhouse. Peter served as a director of both World City Corporation and World City Foundation and had this to say about the World City project:

> It is my expectation that *PHOENIX WORLD CITY* — as a unique resort and sea destination — will attract a major segment of the international travelling public in its varied leisure, conference, business and educational pursuits. As a global forum and international business and cultural center, the range of World City's objectives — beyond travel and leisure — will match the physical magnitude of the project and will represent an important advance in the resort development and travel industries. *PHOENIX WORLD CITY* is, in my opinion, only a beginning, only the first in a new generation of floating resorts which will revolutionize the cruise and travel industry in the years ahead. Its potential for profitability is formidable.

The city-ship, at 255,000 gross registered tons (a measure of cubic space), was designed to a size and capacity that can amply accommodate 5,600 guests (6,200, including children), as well as a crew of 2,600. It is slightly larger than a Nimitz-class aircraft carrier with a beam of 244 feet at the main deck, and a length overall of 1,235 feet. In addition to the three distinctive hotel towers, the ship houses an array of facilities including 100,000 square feet of dedicated meeting, conference and exhibition space, a 2,000-seat theatre and concert hall. Executives, meeting attendees or "Type A" vacationers will have support 24/7 in the ship's business and communications center. There will be a multiplex cinema, sports arena, spa and fitness center, hospital, and wellness clinic. For art enthusiasts, the ship will boast a world-class arts center affiliated with a major land-based arts institution offering rotating exhibits from around the world. A television broadcast studio and media center will ensure that the ship's cultural, educational, philanthropic and business activities are shared with millions ashore, leveraging their impact. There are several exciting nightclubs being planned, including a 350-seat cabaret which will host popular bands, soloists, and comedians. As at any great resort, there will be numerous indoor and outdoor pools, lovely gardens, parks and promenades.

Guests may choose to dine in any of the ship's seventeen restaurants, featuring a wide range of cuisines and an ambiance for any mood or occasion. There will be sixteen bars and cafes, numerous public rooms, a library, specialty galleries, classrooms, art and music studios, game rooms, a children's playhouse, a kennel for visiting pets, a wired teen center with a Kids Only Cafe© and over thirty interesting one-of-a-kind shops and boutiques.

The size of this "city-at-sea" — which is in all respects technically feasible and which in fact results in greater stability and resistance to the elements — will provide an uncrowded sense of spaciousness and freedom notwithstanding the large number of guests which the vessel was designed to accommodate. *A great city – a great solitude.*

With a draft of only ten meters, the city-ship will be able to dock at all major ports-of-call but has also been designed to achieve convenient and highly efficient embarkation and disembarkation, whether alongside *or at anchor.* A unique feature of the ship design is a marina situated inside the hull and accessed through a large entrance in the stern of the vessel. The marina will be served by four 400-passenger day cruisers that can shuttle guests to and from various destinations within a 50 mile radius of the Mother ship. With this flexibility, no port is too small, no destination is inaccessible.

One aspect of the World City concept which particularly separates it from and elevates it above other travel, vacation and cruise experiences is the quality and range of onboard programs,

Port within a ship: Massive stern doors in the city-ship open to reveal a large marina which is home port to four 400 passenger high-speed day cruisers which can transport passengers to and from ports of call and other destinations.

events and activities to be offered. The underlying premise is that relaxation and leisure are enhanced by purposeful activity; that curiosity, creativity and spontaneity thrive in a congenial and relaxed environment; and that understanding and cooperation result as much when people relax and socialize together as when they work and plan together — and even more so when they do both.

For individual visitors and families, *PHOENIX WORLD CITY* will represent the opportunity to gain knowledge and perspective, to share experiences and to be exposed to new ideas and higher goals. For executives, managers, and administrators, it is the chance to sharpen skills and learn new ones, to deepen their awareness of and sensitivity to global concerns, to rub elbows with their peers in diverse fields of endeavor, and to search for new and better directions. For world leaders, decision makers, planners, problem solvers, teachers, artists, writers and scientists, World City is fertile ground in which important seeds can be planted, nurtured and cross-fertilized. In sum, Knut's aim is to create an open and independent cultural and intellectual forum where creativity and new thinking can flourish. Utopia? No, but an opportunity to participate, contribute and feel involved.

In fact, what has just been described is, in many ways, what the World Economic Forum ("Davos") and the Aspen Institute have become for corporate and world leaders. Kloster's idea was to include the leisure traveling public and conference attendees in that process, and to help them use their vacation time or business meetings in a more productive, personally fulfilling and meaningful way.

The city-ship was designed to compete successfully as a cruise product and to also attract two larger markets, the general leisure travel market and the meeting and convention market. As Kloster predicted and pioneered, the trend in the cruise industry shows increasing popularity for larger ships, which are destinations in and of themselves, and shorter itineraries closer to home. Extensive market research confirms that the city-ship concept will attract a significant share of the current cruise market because of the uniqueness of the vessel, the diversity of activities offered and the extensive facilities, services and amenities available.

A major U.S. market, also of growing significance in Europe and Asia, is the business and professional convention and conference market. The World City ship is designed to have particular appeal for international non-profit associations, organizations and membership groups whose purposes are business, educational, cultural or scientific in nature. Because of the extended facilities required for even a medium-sized convention, conference or symposium, by comparison with the limited facilities available on even the larger ships, this enormous market will be drawn to the uniqueness of the city-ship environment which has the ability to keep the conference attendees together, to furnish thousands of comparable guest rooms and suites, and to provide a broader diversity of activities for accompanying spouses and family members, as well as boundless opportunities for recreation, entertainment, wellness and learning.

A part of the World City ship's identity is distinctively a corporate identity, and to maximize the value of the experience for corporate participants World City developed a subscription program whereby 300 of the world's leading corporations are offered an opportunity to lease a corporate suite in the ship's exclusive center hotel tower for a period of five years with renewal rights for an additional five year period. The program is called the "World Class Corporate 300" and it will enable corporate participants to book conference facilities, to help shape the content of executive seminars and other executive programs, and to participate in decisions about World City Foundation's philanthropic activities and grants, leveraging them with their own grant-making when and as they deem appropriate.

Most significantly, World Class Corporate 300 subscriptions provide a financing device which enables the company to use the subscription proceeds, as they are earned from members' use of the ship, to take back equity and reduce debt. This finance scenario greatly enhances the project's ability to increase the quality of onboard programs, improve guest satisfaction and increase the bottom line. At the same time, it provides the means for supporting the company's larger goals and grant-making activities. Again, it is Knut's "2 + 2 = 5" *take* on life.

PHOENIX WORLD CITY, the environment and the common good

It has been Knut's objective from the start that, insofar as it is technically and commercially feasible, the city-ship is to be built and operated in a manner that meets the highest attainable standards of environmental responsibility and serves a higher purpose. World City has worked with participating corporations and governmental agencies to develop and utilize the latest environmentally-sound methods of construction, paying special attention to use of materials, work methods and commitment to innovation. A similar policy has been adopted in connection with the city-ship's operation. The ship's recycling and water treatment programs will ensure that absolutely no refuse or polluted liquids are discharged into the ocean. The ship's use of gas turbines, which utilize a higher grade fuel, will reduce exhaust emissions to levels far below those created by diesel engines which power most currently operating cruise ships. The ship's main engines will operate at the lowest fuel consumption per passenger of any powered commercial ship. Solar energy and other forms of alternative and renewable energy will be adopted for practical as well as demonstration use to the extent feasible.

Nevertheless, there is simply no way around it: *PHOENIX WORLD CITY* will consume fossil fuels. This has troubled Kloster from the very beginning. After incorporating every possible commercially available technology into the design and planned operation of the ship, Knut started thinking of what he could do to ultimately resolve this dilemma. The only answer for a ship this size — nuclear power — raises a new dilemma. Will the public trade long-held but mostly unfounded and irrational fears about nuclear power for a clean, green, zero emission vacation or meeting at sea? This subject is a chapter of its own, Green Clean Global Village®, later on in the book.

In the interim, while that possibility is earnestly explored and hopefully one day in the not too distant future realized, plans for the city-ship as the most environmentally responsible ship on the high seas continue.

"There are a number of reasons to build big, not the least is the ability to save 50% fuel per passenger and similar reductions in polluting waste," Kloster told a reporter from the Norwegian newspaper, *Dagens Næringsliv.* "In this sense, the city-ship is a ship of the future."

Kloster and his partners have reasoned that the resources utilized to create and operate the city-ship will represent a definably minute fraction of the global resources utilized annually for leisure purposes — but in its operation and in the application of it revenues, *PHOENIX WORLD CITY* will represent a major portion of resources devoted to global planning on the part of the private sector and implementation of a sustainable future.

"World City will be tapping into a huge leisure cash flow which," Knut explains, "will, *in any event,* be expended by the populace and which will involve equivalent or greater resource consumption. The major difference is that World City will apply and leverage these financial and physical resources to achieve significant objectives in changing the course of society in areas directly affecting our future and the future of the planet."

"In real effect," he concludes, "the city-ship, over the 30 to 40 years of its life, will return to the earth many-fold what was utilized for its creation and annual operation."

It is Knut's sincere hope that in addition to the influence of the city-ship's programs and activities on passengers and the public, the ship will fully regenerate and *recycle*, for the world's benefit, the full dollar value of the resources which went into its construction and ongoing operation on an average of once every five years.

"The use of the city-ship, in conjunction with World City Foundation and its grant-making initiatives," Knut explained, "will leverage the effect into a series of outreach programs of major international impact."

One of the Foundation's many programmatic ideas, for example, is to annually recruit and train university students from nations around the world in a certificated program, Our Planetary Future©. Every year, a student from every nation in the world would have passed through the six month program and then be sent back to his or her home country with a World City Foundation grant and supporting tools and materials to initiate school and university seminars and tutorials in cooperation with local institutions.

Onboard training programs for the ship's guests and meeting attendees, including the international students participating in the Our Planetary Future© program, will be one part of a continuous series of speakers, seminars and symposia. The value of these educational and training programs will be further leveraged by broad public dissemination via the ship's television and satellite broadcast studio. Printed materials resulting from these onboard programs will be packaged and distributed to the graduates of the certificate program and other participating educational institutions and organizations worldwide.

Just as the "world city" ideal historically represents a reaching out and gathering of the best in the world-*that-is*, Knut hopes that, when realized, his city-ship concept will have a positive impact on our common future and be a catalyst for broader participation in the process.

PHOENIX WORLD CITY, safety and security

The design of the city-ship has set new standards in passenger safety. A revolutionary lifesaving craft and ship evacuation system was developed by Tage Wandborg and reviewed and accepted, in principle, by the Norwegian Maritime Directorate and Det Norske Veritas, the Norwegian classification society. The lifesaving craft and evacuation plan were also reviewed and accepted by the United States Coast Guard (USCG) and the American Bureau of Shipping (ABS).

Twenty large 400-passenger lifesaving craft (ten on each side of the vessel) provide convenient and efficient passenger evacuation in the event of an emergency. Unlike all existing lifeboats, World City's lifesaving craft will be fully enclosed and ventilated, and provide for basic comforts with pantries and bathrooms. The lifesaving craft are at all times ready for instant boarding without any handling of equipment. They are suspended below the cantilevered overhang deck (main deck) so as to permit boarding from the deck below directly onto the craft through one of seven doors on each side of the enclosed craft, by contrast with the conventional open lifeboats which must be swung out and then hazardously boarded over the ship's rail. This rapid, safe and convenient boarding feature is a factor in the projected ability to evacuate all guests and staff in 30 minutes or less. The ship will also have state-of-the art, high-speed boats for rescue operations. In addition, the ship will have a helicopter pad for emergency medical requirements.

A Navy-styled Safety Control Center on board will be staffed continuously. High pressure water curtains, fire alarm systems and fire fighting controls are located in this center. Basic fire indication systems are located throughout the ship and are supplemented by infrared fire detectors where additional safety is required. All public rooms will have sprinkler systems. The vessel will have nine fire zones.

World City's security system complies with, and far surpasses, all U.S. and international rules, regulations and procedures, including "new" proposals — many based on the safety and security features designed into the city-ship by Tage Wandborg and his team.

CHAPTER FIVE
Hands Across the Sea

The American Flagship Project

Although an idealist, Kloster is also a pragmatist and a realist. In his typical maverick and forward-looking style, and despite his Norwegian shipping roots and loyalties, he saw a dynamic business opportunity in a revival of an American Flag passenger ship industry. After all, up to 90% of the $20 billion+ annual cruise revenues are generated by selling tickets to American passengers, and a vast majority of cruises sail out of U.S. ports. Knut therefore decided that his city-ship concept should be taken to America where the ship would be built and operated under the Stars & Stripes.

Building the ship in the U.S. was a decision that would require great daring, involve enormous risk and set Kloster up against the powerful foreign-flag industry he himself had pioneered. It was a decision that would cost him years of delay, millions of dollars and endless bureaucratic backtracking. But when the ship is successfully constructed, it will dramatically grow the industry, have an enormous impact on the U.S. economy, and set a new high standard for the hospitality industry — showing that pleasure and purpose, and profit and higher goals, can co-exist and prosper. Doing well by doing good. Doing what is right, and for the right reasons.

It is possible, but not likely, that if Knut and the rest of his team on the other side of the Atlantic had anticipated the *true* breadth of the American Flagship challenge and the enormous obstacles that would have to be overcome before contracting the world's largest ship in the United States, he *may* have had second thoughts. It is true, however, that neither Knut nor his U.S. colleagues had anticipated how difficult it would be, or that the foreign-flag lobby representing essentially *non-U.S.* interests would be so powerful in Washington under both the Clinton and Bush Administrations to successfully block the entry of an American flag venture from capturing a share of the booming and predominantly

1. **Alabama** — Heart of Dixie
2. **Alaska** — The Last Frontier
3. **Arizona** — Grand Canyon State
4. **Arkansas** — Land of Opportunity
5. **California** — Golden State
6. **Colorado** — Centennial State
7. **Connecticut** — Constitution State
8. **Delaware** — Diamond State
9. **Florida** — Sunshine State
10. **Georgia** — Peach State
11. **Hawaii** — Aloha State
12. **Idaho** — Gem State
13. **Illinois** — Prairie State
14. **Indiana** — Hoosier State
15. **Iowa** — Hawkeye State
16. **Kansas** — Sunflower State
17. **Kentucky** — Bluegrass State
18. **Louisiana** — Pelican State
19. **Maine** — Pine Tree State
20. **Maryland** — Old Line State
21. **Massachusetts** — Bay State
22. **Michigan** — Wolverine State
23. **Minnesota** — Land of 10,000 Lakes
24. **Mississippi** — Magnolia State
25. **Missouri** — Show Me State
26. **Montana** — Treasure State
27. **Nebraska** — Cornhusker State
28. **Nevada** — Silver State
29. **New Hampshire** — Granite State
30. **New Jersey** — Garden State
31. **New Mexico** — Land of Enchantment
32. **New York** — Empire State
33. **North Carolina** — Tar Heel State
34. **North Dakota** — Sioux State
35. **Ohio** — Buckeye State
36. **Oklahoma** — Sooner State
37. **Oregon** — Beaver State
38. **Pennsylvania** — Keystone State
39. **Rhode Island** — Ocean State
40. **South Carolina** — Palmetto State
41. **South Dakota** — Coyote State
42. **Tennessee** — Volunteer State
43. **Texas** — Lone Star State
44. **Utah** — Beehive State
45. **Vermont** — Green Mountain State
46. **Virginia** — The Old Dominion
47. **Washington** — Evergreen State
48. **West Virginia** — Mountain State
49. **Wisconsin** — Badger State
50. **Wyoming** — Equality State

U.S.-based cruise market.

There is no need to dwell on the political aspects of all this because, again, Kristoffer Garin has covered it well in his *Devils on the Deep Blue Sea*, particularly the chapter entitled *"Hiding in Plain Sight"* that gives an inkling of what goes on in the nation's capitol on *both* sides of the aisle. We hear of powerful U.S. special interests but how about powerful non-U.S. interests? The foreign-flag cruise industry is absolutely the best example of that strange and curiously successful breed of power-brokering.

With a new Administration and the U.S. economy reeling from the economic downturn, it is likely that U.S. interests, specifically economic growth and job creation (not to mention a reduction in the nation's record high trade deficit) will trump lobbyists and foreign interests on this round. The timing for the realization of the American Flagship Project could not possibly be better.

Giving back – and other good reasons to build the prototype city-ship in the U.S.

Kloster's reasons for deciding to embark on the American flag initiative were, again, a mix of pragmatism, realism, vision, sentiment and opportunity. From the beginning, he recognized that the United States had welcomed the foreign-flag cruise industry to its shores, and those foreign-flag companies, including NCL, had made their fortunes as a result. Of course, the U.S. economy benefits from the foreign-flag cruise industry, but there is also a compelling opportunity for America to seize a share of this booming market that is operating, to a large extent, on its shores and collecting huge American dollar revenues from American passengers. With a U.S.-built ship, the United States would benefit from a rebirth of commercial passenger ship construction, reap enormous tax benefits and create thousands of new jobs.

In deciding to undertake the American Flagship project, Knut was well aware of the fact that because most of the passengers are American, the foreign-flag cruise industry had become one of the *top ten* contributors to the United States' record high trade deficit, along with *countries* such as Japan, Germany, Mexico and China. It was only a matter of time, he reasoned, before U.S. politicians and the taxpaying public would awaken to this disturbing reality and want to claim a piece of the pie.

The industry was huge and growing steadily. "There's enough business for everyone," Knut said. Even though only a very small percentage of the potential market has taken a cruise, the industry represents the fastest growing segment of the leisure travel industry. John F. Kennedy said, and Knut agrees, "a rising tide lifts all ships."

"The American Flagship project has an enormous potential to benefit the industry as a whole, the American economy in particular, and the larger leisure travel industry generally," Knut argues.

Another reason that Knut decided on the American Flagship project was because, under the American flag, the city-ship could trade along America's coastline, visiting ports-of-call along the way, and enabling tremendous flexibility in the guests' length of stay. Under the Passenger Vessel Services Act (PVSA), coastwise trading is (theoretically) reserved to U.S.-built and U.S.-flagged [registered] vessels. Most maritime countries also have such cabotage laws to protect domestic trading. There are similar laws in the airline business.

With coastwise itineraries and the added flexibility provided by the day cruisers, guests would be able to check in and check out at will, just as they do at any hotel or resort. This increases turnover, which is where the profits are made in this highly competitive industry.

Kloster recognized that to attract first-time cruisers, the meeting and conference market, and the larger general leisure travel market, passengers must have greater flexibility in terms of length of stay. They need to be able to come aboard for one day, two days, three days, or however long they wish. One of the drawbacks of a conventional cruise is the need to commit to a 7-day or longer cruise (although this is changing as the foreign-flag industry continues to erode U.S. cabotage laws, discussed below, and in more detail in Garin's book).

Kloster further realized that, as ships become ever larger, they will be, like *PHOENIX WORLD CITY,* destinations in and of themselves, and guests will increasingly choose the cruise experience as a way to just get away, to participate in a broad range of recreational, cultural and educational programs and activities and enjoy an array of entertainment, shopping, dining and other pleasures without having to travel very far to get there and without having to commit to a long voyage or visit an increasingly overcrowded Caribbean destination.

Recognizing that the city-ship was designed to also attract the meeting and conference market, it is important to position the ship where meeting attendees can easily get to it, and leave when they choose to leave (as opposed to when the ship returns to port). Under the American flag, the ship will trade, for example, from New York in the spring, summer and fall, and from Port Canaveral in the winter months, which, taken together, encompasses 25 metropolitan areas and 12 of the nation's and the world's largest tourist destinations, attracting a population of 100 million Americans within an hour's drive of a place where they can get on or off the ship. Moreover, only meetings conducted on American-flagged vessel are eligible for tax deductibility under U.S. law.

As the cruise pioneer and innovator, Kloster was also considering ways to circumvent the cyclical nature of the hospitality industry in general and the cruise industry in particular. All resorts and cruise lines experience varying degrees of seasonality which affect occupancy as well as room rates. The high season in a given market segment is usually only four months. In order to keep occupancy up year-round, cruise lines and hotel/resort operators commonly discount room rates or offer upgrades or other incentives to attract guests during the low season.

Under the American flag, the city-ship could be positioned to attract markets which have their peak seasons at different times of the year — accessing those markets in their respective peak seasons — *year round.* Knut recognized that this flexibility, available only on a coastwise domestic itinerary — reserved under law to U.S.-built, U.S.-flagged vessels — would enable the city-ship to maintain high season occupancy *and* room rates throughout the year.

With the end of the cold war, and a great deal of talk at the time on the part of U.S. politicians about "downsizing" the navy and converting to dual-use (military and commercial) technologies, Kloster and his U.S. partners anticipated that they would be welcomed with open arms by the major U.S. defense-dependent shipyards. While this open-arm reception never materialized, it was one of the reasons Knut initially embarked on the Build America scenario. An even better reason to build in the United States was the availability of low-interest, long-term government loan guarantees for shipowners with economically sound projects who agreed to build their ships in the United States and to operate them under the American flag, thus promoting the U.S. Merchant Marine and enhancing the country's manufacturing infrastructure.

In sum, going with U.S. construction and the American flag seemed to Knut to be a perfect opportunity all around and a great way to attract the additional new markets which the city-ship was designed to serve, while giving back to the citizens of a country that spurred the growth of this industry in the first place.

Knut fully recognized that a conventional-size cruise ship could not compete in the U.S. market as an American flag operation because, under the American flag, the owning company would have to pay U.S. corporate and payroll taxes and abide by generally more stringent (and therefore more costly) labor, safety and environmental "rules of the road." Those competitive disadvantages would be offset by the city-ship's much larger size that permits more profit centers than on conventional cruise ships (i.e., greatly expanded shopping, dining, learning, gaming, spa, wellness and self-enrichment opportunities). The flexible, closer-to-home, coastwise itineraries, and the ability to check in and check out at will — *theoretically* possible only under a U.S.-flag operation — would greatly increase guest turnover and, therefore, volume of discretionary spending.

To take advantage of this opportunity, Kloster entered into a contract with John S. Rogers, a prominent New York admiralty attorney and longtime friend, under which a new U.S. corporation was formed to own and operate the prototype American flag vessel. It was agreed that the profits of the ship, after endowing World City Foundation and the larger goals that Knut and John shared, would be apportioned between Oslo, New York and other U.S. shareholders[4].

At the suggestion of Hon. Helen Delich Bentley, former Chairman of the U.S. Federal Maritime Commission and five-term member of The United States House of Representatives, the prototype American Flagship would be named *AMERICA WORLD CITY*. Thus, World City America Inc., World City Foundation (NY),

---

[4] To operate under an American flag and to qualify for federal loan guarantees, U.S.-built ships must be owned 75% by U.S. interests.

The Hon. Helen Delich Bentley, former Chairman of the Federal Maritime Commission and 5-term Member of Congress (R-MD) and Knut Utstein Kloster raise a glass to the American Flagship Project.

Knut announces his decision to take the Phoenix project to America.

and the American Flagship project were born.

A "National Collaborative" was formed to bring together dozens of major U.S. Fortune 500 Corporations who stood to benefit from the realization of an American-flag cruise ship industry — including GE, Du Pont, AT&T, United Technologies, 3M, Alcoa, Delta Airlines and many more. As an independent, non-partisan, not-for-profit organization, The Build America Committee, was created to promote the construction of the ship in the United States, and the former President of the Massachusetts Maritime Academy, Admiral John (Jack) Aylmer, was brought on as Executive Director. The objectives of the Committee were threefold:

- to energize the personal involvement of leaders from business, labor, government and media in support of America's bid to construct the city-ship in the United States and to promote operation of the ship under the American flag

- to maximize use of American technology, products and services from all fifty states in the building, outfitting and operation of the ship
- to provide a unique platform for a broader "Build America" initiative — one which will promote recognition of the resourcefulness and productivity inherent in the U.S. economy and serve as a catalyst for the renewal of America's industrial and commercial preeminence and its confidence as a nation.

A "Build America Caucus" was formed on Capitol Hill, consisting of over a 120 members of Congress. The Build America Caucus was quick to recognize the enormous benefits to be derived from creation of an American flag cruise industry, including the following benefits that would flow from just the first in a series of next generation city-ships:

- $1.5 billion in construction, outfitting and supplies for U.S. companies
- over 10 million work hours for U.S. workers
- construction contracts valued at $500 million for the State of Florida
- $350 million in contracts for the States of Mississippi and Louisiana; $250 million for the State of Texas; and $150 million in additional components, systems and supplies procured from every state in the union
- 2,600 onboard jobs for American officers, crew and hospitality staff, and thousands of jobs ashore
- over $4.5 billion in direct tax revenues over the life of a Title XI loan guarantee
- over $300 million in maintenance and repair contracts over the life of the ship operating on a coastwise itinerary out of Port Canaveral, Florida, in the winter months and New York in the spring, fall and summer, the estimated annual impact on U.S. ports and coastal communities is over $500 million
- new levels of productivity and competitiveness for the U.S. maritime industry
- balance of trade improvements
- the psychological boost to public confidence from the nation embarking on an optimistic, forward-looking, entrepreneurial project, involving a cross section of American industry, to claim for Americans a role in a major high-profile market.

A "Black Caucus" also was formed to help identify and capture opportunities for African-American businesses, large and small, and to create jobs in construction and hospitality for African-American citizens, including training programs for disadvantaged youth.

Mindful of the benefits of America's entry into the booming cruise sector, the United States Congress appropriated $15 million in the FY '93 Defense Appropriations Act for research and development funding for the American Flagship project. The Conference Report issued by Hon. Bob Livingston of Louisiana stated:

> Mr. Speaker, the conference report on H.R. 5504, the fiscal year 1993 Defense Appropriations Act expressed the concern of the conferees over the general decline in the health of the American shipbuilding industry. As one of the provisions for defense conversion, the conferees directed that $15 million be utilized to establish and implement viable opportunities for conversion of the defense-oriented shipbuilding industry to market driven commercial production activities, help maintain the defense industrial base, and further the development and maintenance of an adequate merchant marine. This action was based on requests by leading U.S. shipyards, corporations and other organizations, including the American Bureau of Shipping, for applied research and development funding to assist them in undertaking construction in the United States of the largest passenger ship in the world, *PHOENIX WORLD CITY*. The ship would be the first passenger ship built in this country in over 40 years, and it is projected to be the first of a fleet of three such ships which will fly the American Flag and operate, manned by American crews, on both coasts and in Hawaii. While the impact of this national project will be nationwide, a number of yards in my State and along the Gulf Coast are already actively involved and thousands of Louisiana shipyard workers could directly benefit from the R & D program earmarked in H.R. 5504 and the possible construction work that could follow. This project may have important economic significance not only for the shipbuilding industry, but for corporations across the Nation, for our merchant marine, and for domestic ports and tourism. I believe that it was the intention of the conferees that these funds be utilized to help

bring the American shipbuilding industry to a point at which
this major ship construction project can be realized in U.S.
shipyards and the industry thereby positioned to address
other commercial opportunities that will surely follow.

In the first of many setbacks to be experienced, the American
Flagship project did not receive the FY 93 Defense Appropriations
R & D funding. With a change in the administration from President
Bush to President Clinton, and political restructuring common
after a change of administration, the monies were rolled over into
President Clinton's Technology Reinvestment Program (TRP). World
City America, obviously disappointed, nonetheless bounced back,
putting together one of the most comprehensive teams in American
history in support of its TRP proposal: "A National Shipbuilding
Initiative: Phase Zero."

The team included the American Bureau of Shipping (ABS);
the United States Navy; the Agile Manufacturing Enterprise Forum
(AMEF) of the Iacocca Institute at Lehigh University; Concurrent
Technologies Corporation; twelve of the nation's major defense
and commercial shipyards, including Newport News, Avondale
and Ingalls; Odense Steel Shipyard in Denmark (for 3D modeling);
dozens of U.S. corporations including DuPont, AT&T, General
Electric, ALCOA, 3M, Caterpillar and Westinghouse; six major
universities including M.I.T., Clemson, Tufts, the University
of Alabama and the University of New Orleans; and dozens of
technology providers from across the country.

Kloster was very proud of World City America's ability to put
together such an impressive team to compete for R & D funding
under President Clinton's TRP "jobs" program, but, as he would
eventually discover, the workings of the U.S. political system are
much more complex and complicated than meet the eye. This was

only the beginning of Knut's sad awakening to the reality of U.S. politics, pork and lobbying. World City did not receive *any* of the TRP funding. Equally disappointing in terms of the potential benefits to the U.S. economy, the TRP "jobs" program did not turn out to be a successful "jobs" program either.

This is one of the greatest challenges of the Obama Administration — to insure that the billions invested in the stimulus program *actually create and save jobs.* There is no better, lower risk, ready-to-go, privately developed, job-creating national project of the same scale and potential economic impact as the American Flagship project. After GM's high profile bankruptcy and the State of the Union in other manufacturing sectors, the American Flagship project would provide the boost in morale and confidence needed to remind America: YES WE CAN.

The American Flagship Construction Program

World City carried on without any government support. An American technical team was assembled, including the former Commandant of the United States Coast Guard, Admiral J. William Kime, to direct all aspects of the ship's safety and compliance with U.S. Coast Guard regulations. Richard (Dick) Baumler, one of the United States' most experienced marine engineers, was brought in as Chief Engineer. Dick has had extensive dealings with and has held top executive positions at several of the major U.S. shipyards and served as Vice President for Ship Construction for Sealand.

The original *PHOENIX* was designed with direct diesel drive propulsion and auxiliary electric generators to develop the 30MW of hotel electrical load. Dick Baumler recommended use of a diesel electric plant since, during most of the operating periods, the hotel

Although President Obama used the "YES WE CAN" slogan in his successful presidential campaign, World City distributed its YES WE CAN flyer to every member of Congress back in 2004 and views it as an appropriate "call to action" for all Americans and for all time.

electrical load was greater than the propulsion power required (25MW). A total propulsion power consisting of four (4) 20 MW electric motors would enable the ship to travel at 21 knots, a speed requirement suggested by the U.S. Navy so that the ship could be deemed to have "military significance" in the event of national emergency such as hurricane evacuation, as hospital ship or as troop carrier.

While it is important to demonstrate the ship's military usefulness in a national emergency, which carries several benefits including a statutory preference for government loan guarantees, the actual cruising speed contemplated during normal ship operations is from 8 to 15 knots.

The reconfigured design was submitted by World City America Inc. to Avondale Shipyard in Louisiana. Avondale was to work side-by-side with World City's technical team and in close cooperation with the United States Coast Guard and American Bureau of Shipping to prepare a ship specification and contract plans that were required

Left to right: Knut Kloster, Tage Wandborg, John Rogers, Dick Baumler and Jim Dolan (ABS), showing the ship model at a Society of Naval Architects and Marine Engineers (SNAME) conference.

for U.S. shipyard bid purposes.

All necessary Damage Stability, Fire Segregations, Structural Analysis and Critical System Analysis were conducted at Avondale. They were also to submit a cost proposal for building the ship at their facilities.

Avondale's bid proved to be uncompetitive and therefore unworkable. A detailed analysis of the bid revealed that the principal cost drivers related to Avondale's prolonged build schedule and the outfitting of the hotel components, an area in which Avondale (and all U.S. shipyards) lacked experience.

When the marine gas turbines developed by GE for naval ship use were later offered for commercial ship application, World City immediately recognized the environmental, safety and space advantages of gas turbines over diesel engines and modified the ship's design accordingly. Several other cruise lines subsequently specified gas turbines for power and electric propulsion but none of the cruise companies have thus far eliminated diesel engines.

The Virtual Shipyard

A "virtual shipyard" replaces the vertical integration of a traditional yard with integration among multiple yards, and their suppliers and subcontractors, in a manner that supports and enhances current concepts of modular ship design and construction through electronic interface, uniform application of best practices, responsiveness to market requirements, and allocation of work among participating entities according to core competencies.

After a sizable investment of time and money, it was sadly concluded that the U.S. defense-dependent shipyards were unable, or possibly unwilling, to develop commercially competitive standards and practices and were not viable contenders for construction of the American Flagship. Nonetheless, World City America worked with a number of these defense-dependent shipyards for several years, including Avondale, Newport News and General Dynamics, in developing the engineering package for the ship and benefited in that respect from the association.

With the conclusion that the nation's large defense-reliant shipyards would be unable (or unwilling) to build the ship on a commercially viable basis, and with Avondale's unfeasible bid, World City developed a modular construction scenario — literally a "virtual shipyard" — whereby the work is divided among several construction entities, including a major land based hotel contractor, Centex Construction.[5]

In a 21st century application of the multi-yard and modular construction concepts conceived by Henry Kaiser to produce the famed fleet of Liberty Ships in World War II, World City America assembled a cross-section of U.S. commercial shipbuilding, offshore and general construction expertise and resources for construction of the prototype city-ship. It was the first application of the "virtual shipyard" concept increasingly common in European passenger ship construction.

Although the United States had not built a major passenger ship in nearly half a century, and despite widespread skepticism, Kloster and the team he had assembled for the American Flagship project, under John S. Rogers, had no doubt whatsoever that the United States of America had the industrial resources and expertise to accomplish the task of engineering and constructing the city-ship, and doing so on an internationally competitive basis.

---

[5] Centex has since become Balfour Beatty Construction, and some key members of the Centex team assigned to this project formed a new and highly successful entity, Moss & Associates. It is the intention of World City America Inc. to continue to focus on people and their core competencies in putting the final hotel construction team together.

(Seated) Bob Moss, then Chairman and CEO of Centex, with John S. Rogers, Chairman and CEO of World City America Inc., flanked by members of the build team, Chief Architect, Tage Wandborg (second from right), and some "visitors" from a leading Finnish shipyard [separate story, told at the end of this chapter].

Chief Architect Tage Wandborg demonstrates how the modules of the ship's hull and superstructure will be joined together.

Captain Warren Leback, former U.S. Maritime Administrator and also an advisor to World City, announced that "the innovative manner of constructing the city-ship will be as revolutionary as the product itself; the work will be undertaken by a consortium which will combine the skills and resources of the nation's shipbuilding industry with those of the highly

U.S. Maritime Administrator at the time, Captain Warren Leback, holds up model of the city-ship at MARAD headquarters in Washington, D.C.

Chief Architect Tage Wandborg illustrates virtual shipyard concept at a Defense Manufacturing Conference.

competitive U.S. offshore and hotel construction industries."

Former United States Coast Guard Commandant, Admiral J. William Kime, became the Chairman of the American Flagship Construction Company (AFCC) that will serve as prime contractor for the virtual shipyard consortium.

It was decided that it would be far easier to teach a land-based hotel contractor marine standards, specifications and structural requirements — which relate primarily to the use of fire safe materials and vibration issues — than to teach a defense-reliant shipyard how to be commercially competitive. The hotel construction team worked for a year with Tage Wandborg, the

United States Coast Guard and the American Bureau of Shipping and determined that it could build the superstructure and outfit the passenger accommodations on a competitive basis, to marine standards, both in terms of cost and schedule. In many respects, this was similar to what Centex and other successful hotel builders had been doing throughout the Caribbean and southern United States in building resorts to hurricane specification.

Under the innovative "virtual shipyard" construction concept, the hull modules will be built in a number of commercial shipyards in the Gulf region and barged to an assembly site near Corpus Christi, Texas. Kiewit Offshore Services was selected for the complex hull assembly and final outfitting based on its extensive experience in fabricating and assembling huge offshore structures, as well as Kiewit's outstanding safety record and on-time/on-budget performance.

Randall Wroblewski, who started out with World City as a Merchant Marine Academy Intern and who later earned an MBA in Finance, contributed enormously over the years to the project's business development, including assisting in the preparation of World City's Title XI application. Randy is seen here in World City's New York office with the company's voluminous Title XI application the day it was submitted to MARAD.

Simultaneous with the hull construction, the hotel modules will be constructed at a dedicated build site in Port Canaveral, Florida — the ship's future homeport. The hotel modules were designed and arranged to utilize required fire zone separations which would permit the complete outfitting of the hotel spaces in the modular stage prior to erection.

Ultimately, the completed hull will be sailed around from Texas to Port Canaveral where the fully outfitted hotel modules will be skidded aboard. The ship's three deck "downtown" area will then be "stick built" on board, much like the construction of a mall ashore. The entire build cycle will take approximately 36 months — about half the time estimated by Avondale — and the total cost will be competitive, on both a per passenger and per ton basis, with subsidized passenger ship facilities in Europe.

Tage Wandborg and Dick Baumler visited several of the commercial shipyards in the Gulf Coast region to determine how each might participate in the construction of the hull modules. Pro forma construction contracts were entered into and a comprehensive Title XI Loan Guarantee Application was prepared and submitted to the United States Maritime Administration (MARAD), costing several million dollars.

To meet MARAD requirements, World City America Inc. put together over $300 million in vendor financing and equity commitments from strategic partners including GE, Caterpillar and Siemens USA.

World City America retained Marsh Inc. to review its construction plan. After a year-long study, including meetings with all participants, the United States Coast Guard, the American Bureau of Shipping and the United States Maritime Administration, Marsh concluded that World City's "virtual shipyard" plan — which will compete in cost and build time with European shipyard construction — will be completed on time and on budget. Marsh offered World City a $1.3 billion Financial Protection Program which essentially guarantees the U.S. government and project investors that the ambitious and innovative plan *will* succeed. This protection would be over and above normal construction bonding on the part of the build team.

World City America Inc. entered into a contract with Westin Hotels & Resorts to market and manage the ship and with Grand Casinos, Inc. to handle the gaming operations on board. World City selected Westin because it is one of the oldest and most respected hospitality operators in the country and a leading upscale brand. At the time the deal was made with Grand Casinos, it was one of the largest and most successful gaming companies in the United States. Both Westin and Grand Casinos also made equity commitments.

After the management contract with Westin had been entered into, the hotel chain became part of Starwood Hotels and Resorts Worldwide, but maintained its own brand identity. The association with Starwood added to Westin's marketing clout.

Lyle Berman, who was one of the founders of Grand Casinos, Inc., and the company's Chairman and CEO, later merged the company with Hilton Gaming to become Park Place Entertainment, but Lyle did not include the World City contract in the merger and

Left to right: Tage Wandborg, John Rogers, Stephanie Gallagher, Juergen Bartels [then Westin's Chairman and CEO] and Knut at announcement of World City's association with Westin Hotels & Resorts

will operate the shipboard casino under Lakes Gaming, Inc. Mr. Berman is a principal owner of Lakes Gaming as well as its Chairman and CEO.

The Linear City Concept

After an extensive study of possible home ports for the American Flagship, conducted by Bechtel, World City selected Port Canaveral in Central Florida to be the future homeport of the prototype ship. Many scoffed at the idea, since the port was, at that time, just getting into the cruise sector. World City recognized that the port had tremendous growth potential and an ambitious and visionary leadership under Charles (Chuck) Rowland, as Executive Director, and Joe La Polla as Deputy Director and Port Engineer. Chuck and Joe were also supported by a board of outstanding commissioners who recognized the port's potential and were determined to make Port Canaveral one of the greatest cruise ports in the world. That's exactly what has happened in the interim.

To support and enhance its selection of Port Canaveral as the ideal homeport for the city-ship, World City proposed the creation of an unprecedented international "Linear City" between Orlando International Airport and Port Canaveral. The Linear City would represent a balanced integration of residential, high-tech industrial, resort, leisure and recreational elements, all linked — internally and to the world — by a modern network of utilities, communications and high-speed transportation. The proposed Linear City, as a whole and in each of its components will be a major attraction, a model of community, industrial and environmental planning, and a significant service to the surrounding regions. The Greater Orlando Aviation Authority, the Orlando Utilities Commission and the City of Orlando joined the Canaveral Port Authority in endorsing the Linear City project.

To prove the viability of the plan, World City secured temporary options on all required land rights, including those from the Mormons who control a vast amount of property used as farmland east of the Orlando International Airport. The Linear City remains an integral part of the American Flagship project.

International Council of Cruise Lines (ICCL) lobbies U.S. Congress

Although Knut anticipated *some* resistance from the foreign-flag cruise industry to the American Flagship project, he and John Rogers definitely underestimated the opposition that would be mounted by the industry.

It was more than the fact that the city-ship had the very real potential to raise customer expectation beyond a level that the existing foreign-flag fleet could hope to meet, though that was, of course, a legitimate concern. The foreign-flag cruise industry had its own eyes on the advantages of a U.S. coastwise itinerary and the resulting ability to offer shorter cruises to increase turnover and revenues and to attract first-time cruisers. But under the Passenger Vessel Services Act (PVSA), this is not (theoretically) permissible.

The PVSA was enacted to ensure that American domestic coastal water trade routes (i.e., transportation of passengers from one U.S. port to another), like every other domestic industry and means of transportation, are reserved to companies that are subject to the full thrust of U.S. labor, tax, immigration, environmental and workplace laws and standards.

The Secretary of Commerce applies a "domestic commerce" test to PVSA, holding that a voyage on which passengers boarded a German ship in New York, traveled around the world visiting seventeen foreign ports and disembarked in San Francisco, was not "domestic commerce" coming within the prohibition of the Act. He reasoned that the disembarking of the passengers at San Francisco "was a mere incident" to a foreign voyage.

Camel's nose under the tent

Building on that rationale and subsequent Customs' rulings, foreign-flag cruise ships have worked the camel's nose under the tent, gradually eroding both the letter and spirit of the PVSA, as well as blocking one legislative proposal after another aimed at leveling the playing field or facilitating an American participation in this lucrative U.S.-based market.

The foreign-flag fleet now routinely conducts tourism voyages along the U.S. coastline, escaping the PVSA by including a non-U.S. port in the itinerary (e.g., a "fall foliage" itinerary from New York to multiple New England ports, ending in Halifax, Nova Scotia). It apparently has not yet occurred to the U.S. authorities that *tourism*, not transportation to the foreign port, is the commercial activity being engaged in and that such voyages obviously constitute "domestic commerce" in competition with American travel and hospitality industries.

Having, figuratively, gotten their nose under the tent, the foreign-flag cruise fleet now regularly sails up and down America's east and west coastlines, in Hawaii, and in Alaska, having only to add a foreign port to theoretically legitimize the activity. For example, using the "foreign port" rationalization, a number of cruise lines are offering year-round Hawaiian itineraries which call at four major Hawaiian islands, offering 23 Hawaiian shore excursions, and escaping the reach of the PVSA under U.S. Customs' interpretations by sailing to and calling for a few hours (if that) at the sparsely populated Fanning Island in the Republic of Kiribati. Similarly, ships trade out of San Francisco and Los Angeles by calling for a few hours (if that) at Ensenada, Mexico and offer multi-port Alaskan cruises by calling at Vancouver.

But the foreign-flag cruise industry would rather not be bound, at all, with the need to continue the pretense of "foreign travel" or be required to add that foreign port-of-call to their otherwise domestic itineraries. It has, for a long time, been a top priority of the well-funded foreign-flag cruise industry lobby to get the PVSA changed or repealed. The cruise lines deny this while continuing to use their powerful lobbying clout, and that of various ports currently benefiting from the cruise industry, to make steady headway on this objective in Washington.

Bob Dickinson, the former President of Carnival Cruise Lines, basically admitted that the cruise lines are taking a back seat in the battle, solely for appearance's sake:

> The cruise industry has been, by design, a bit of a bystander on this particular issue, only because we sense that... this is one that we're not going to win on our own. The port cities and port states have far more political clout than we do. They're the ones who are leading the fight.[6]

In a *Time Magazine*[7] interview, Dickinson also conceded the point that the cruise lines are not in the transportation business at all, but rather in direct competition with U.S. hotels, resorts, and vacation destinations:

---

[6] Source: *Journal of Commerce*, April 19, 1996
[7] *Time Magazine*, June 1997

At the mass end of the market, however, cruise ships are entering an era when they must compete with land resorts in terms of price, entertainment and amenities. 'We see ourselves as a vacation business, rather than a cruise business,' says Dickinson, and he acknowledges that his competition increasingly is Las Vegas and Disney.

In a news release from Royal Caribbean announcing the construction of one of its giant new ships, it was conceded that the ship would "boast meeting and conference space rivaling or exceeding that of many land-based conference facilities" and will be "a total vacation experience equal to — perhaps even better than — the best land-based alternative." Doesn't that sound a little like Knut's city-ship project?

An American flag entrant into the booming cruise market, especially the world's largest cruise ship, was seen as a real threat to the cruise lines' long-held (albeit denied) political objective regarding domestic coastwise trading. World City America Inc. found itself consumed in the double challenge of doing what many in the cruise business said was impossible — building the world's largest passenger ship in the United States which had not built a major passenger ship in nearly half a century — and fighting a rear guard attack by the foreign-flag cruise industry's lobbying organization. The process was, at best, awkward for Knut, but he never waivered in his steadfast conviction that what he was trying to do would be good for the cruise industry, good for the travelling public, good for the American economy and destined to ultimately be a huge success which would be good for World City's shareholders and strategic partners and for the company's larger goals as well.

American Flagship "Campaign"

As Knut recognized when he decided that the prototype city-ship should be built in the United States and operated under the American flag, the foreign cruise fleet had become a leading contributor to America's record high trade deficit. Surprisingly, when World City America Inc. began its "Build America" campaign, most members of Congress mistakenly thought the cruise industry was an "American industry," paying U.S. corporate taxes, hiring Americans and bound by U.S. labor "rules of the road".

Nor were many legislators aware of the actual *size* of the industry which, by the mid-nineties, had greater revenues than the nation's entire annual motion picture box office, the gate of America's four largest professional sports, and the total revenues of all Walt Disney and Universal Studios theme parks *combined.*

Former Coast Guard Commandant, Admiral J. William Kime, and World City America Inc. Chairman and CEO, John S. Rogers, pose with the Clintons at the White House. On this occasion, John Rogers asked the First Lady if she would be the Godmother of the American Flagship. The former First Lady graciously accepted.

Obviously, this was a major business opportunity for the U.S. maritime and hospitality industries. World City America Inc. and the National Collaborative of U.S. corporations it had enlisted began a widespread mail, media and advertising campaign to awaken Americans and their legislators to the fact that America should be capturing a share of this predominantly U.S. market for its economy, workers and state and federal tax coffers. Members of the National Collaborative wrote to the Administration and to Congress urging support for the American Flagship project.

In its letter of support, AT&T wrote:

> We applaud the diverse group of skilled American participants, both public and private, which has been assembled to implement this truly national project, and we assure you that AT&T will do its part to realize both the integrated virtual shipyard and a state-of-the-art passenger ship to once again carry the nation's flag in international competition.

GE sent this message to members of Congress who represented Districts in which GE has U.S. operations:

> General Electric Company, one of the world's leading manufacturers of marine electrical and power systems, regards the American Flagship project as a major breakthrough in the use of the oceans for leisure and for business, and is pleased to be a part of this revolution together with other leading U.S. corporations... Also noteworthy is the proposed use of gas turbines on the ship which will help realize World City's objective of creating the most environmentally-friendly ship on the oceans.

Caterpillar's message to Congress and the Administration was right to the point:

> World City represents a major breakthrough for our country, our citizens and the economy… this effort recaptures an industry dominated by foreign-flag vessels through the deployment of U.S. technology.

The President of Massachusetts Maritime Academy wrote the Massachusetts delegation:

> Our highly trained and motivated graduates increasingly find themselves "on the beach" watching foreign ships and crews sail away with U.S. commerce and passengers. This state of affairs need not continue. America can be competitive in both ship construction and operation, demonstrated by the American Flagship project… the Massachusetts Maritime Academy has supported this project from the outset and is proud to have been the first of our nation's maritime academies to enter into a training arrangement for cadets to serve on the ship as part of its onboard training program.

The American Bureau of Shipping (ABS), which is the nation's ship classification society, wrote this:

> The American Flagship project now stands contract-ready with an innovative construction plan — involving a revolutionary "virtual shipyard" that will bring together the best and most competitive that America has to offer in the construction of an historic new ship. We at ABS firmly believe that this enterprise is not only of a magnitude to enlarge the imagination and energies of companies across America as well as agencies of the government, but will stand as a symbol of renewal — an American Flagship with which all Americans can identify.

In an announcement to the Society of Naval Architects and Marine Engineers (SNAME) in November 1995, the United States Coast Guard stated that "World City is one organization which is currently doing it right... this type of partnership with the U.S.C.G. should be the rule rather than the exception."

World City published a series of flyers aimed at educating the public and Congress. The campaign was an enormous success which explains why over 120 Members of Congress and many state governors signed on to the Build America Caucus. Nonetheless, behind the scenes and with a huge lobbying budget, World City America Inc. found itself fighting a steep uphill battle in Washington. It wouldn't prove anything to name names as most of the elected officials whose support may have been dampened by the foreign-flag cruise industry lobby have now moved on. It was a game of "May I?" Two steps forward, one step back, most of the time.

There are hopeful signs that the chances for realization of the project under President Obama's Administration are greatly improved since job creation, reduction in the nation's trade deficit and support of America's manufacturing base are more important than ever in today's gloomy economy.

Why does the World City project need the government's support anyway?

Because the foreign-flag cruise companies start out with a huge competitive advantage, including ship construction subsidies in European shipyards, cheap Third World labor and the fact that the cruise lines operate in the United States virtually free of any of the encumbrances with which U.S. companies must contend, such as state, corporate and payroll taxes, and American laws relating to labor, safety and the environment.[8]

---

[8] Knut understands the economics argument on both sides of the issue and is quick to defend the foreign-flag cruise industry's contribution to the American economy and also to point out that the industry's safety record has been outstanding. Under Knut's leadership at NCL, safety was certainly the paramount consideration.

In Kristoffer A. Garin's book, *The Devils on the Deep Blue Sea*, he calculates that if, for example, Wal-Mart was earning at Carnival's tax-free profit margins in 2003, it would have made an unheard of $65 billion in profits, compared with the $8 billion in income Wal-Mart reported in that year — and paid taxes on. It's far from a level playing field.

The only government assistance which the United States offers U.S. shipowners is the opportunity to apply for low interest, long-term loan guarantees for economically sound shipbuilding projects. The loan guarantee program, called Title XI, is administered by the United States Maritime Administration (MARAD) which, when the American Flagship project was launched, had little acquaintance with the cruise industry or passenger ship construction.

Misguided upstart steals the stage

After World City America Inc. finally inched its way painfully through the MARAD Title XI review process — which took years and cost millions — a competing American-flag initiative entered the fray (dubbing itself "Project America," a copycat initiative to World City's long-planned and arduously developed American Flagship project) with a plan to build two conventional size vessels in a defense-dependent shipyard, Ingalls at Pascagoula, Mississippi — the state and hometown of Senator Trent Lott, then Senate Majority Leader.

Senator Lott had met with World City executives, Admiral Kime, and Honorable Helen Delich Bentley on several occasions, had seen the merits of the American Flagship project, and pledged his support, as did many other members of Congress on both sides of the aisle.

World City had spent millions learning the unfortunate

lesson that U.S. defense-dependent shipyards cannot compete commercially — or do not wish to do so. But by the time American Classic Voyages' "Project America" surfaced with its plan, Ingalls needed work and decided to take on the project. Senator Lott naturally supported — and pushed for — Project America's Title XI application. Since American Classic Voyages planned to operate the ships exclusively in Hawaii, Senator Inouye, the senior senator from that State, also pushed for approval of Project America's application.

World City's extensive market studies had demonstrated that to compete under the American flag with the foreign-flag cruise industry, a highly differentiated product to attract much larger markets than just the cruise market was required.

MARAD (i.e., the U.S. taxpayers) paid most of the $5 million cost of a market study that showed that the projected ships, which were to operate in Hawaii, could not compete with the low cost foreign-flag cruise industry. They *could not compete* even after Congress took the unprecedented step of granting the ships a pre-construction monopoly[9] for their projected Hawaiian operation as a way to offset the reality confirmed by the market study.

Almost overnight, comparatively speaking, the $1.4 billion Title XI loan guarantee was approved for American Classic Voyages. "Project America" was ill-fated from the start, not only because of the uncompetitive method of construction of the vessels in a defense-reliant shipyard, but because of the undistinguished conventional design, size and concept of the vessels themselves. However well-meaning, Congress tried to substitute legislation for the marketability of the Hawaiian-based project, but because of

---

[9] Since the United States cannot dictate the commerce of foreign nations, the monopoly only applied to competition from any American flag vessels, meaning that World City's ships would not be allowed to compete with "Project America" in Hawaiian waters, but, of course, the real competition was the foreign-flag fleet.

loopholes in the Passenger Vessel Services Act, ended up excluding only U.S.-flag competition. Even before the keel was laid for the first vessel, the foreign-flag fleet lined up to eat America's lunch, yet again, by introducing bigger, better, cheaper foreign-built ships with all their low-cost advantages into the Hawaiian domestic trade in direct unfettered competition with the American-flag operator.[10]

"Project America" unfortunately played out just as World City had predicted. Neither ship was completed and the American taxpayers reportedly lost approximately $500 million in the process. This fiasco gave the Title XI program a black eye that would take Congress years to forget. The program has still not been resurrected although there are signs that it will be in the near future.

It was right for MARAD, albeit belatedly, to attempt to facilitate America's entry into the booming cruise sector to take advantage of America's own powerful and growing markets and to encourage introduction of commercial standards and competitive methodologies in American shipbuilding. But it was a mistake for MARAD to ignore the realities of the competition and to imagine that a conventional cruise ship built in a conventional manner by a defense-reliant shipyard with little commercial experience and *no* passenger ship experience, could ever be positioned to compete successfully with the entrenched, low-cost foreign-flag fleet.

On the contrary, and as World City America Inc. had been urging for years, there is a compelling and irresistible market-driven opportunity for the American flag and the American merchant marine in the construction and operation of the next generation of cruise ships to serve America's growing interest in cruising, in

---

[10] As part of the Congressionally granted monopoly to American Classic Voyages, the company was permitted, while the new ships were under construction, to bring in a foreign-built ship and operate it under the American flag — not any more successful than the construction side of the scheme and for the same reasons.

tourism and in meetings-at-sea. However, this opportunity can only be seized by an equally compelling and irresistible product and a common sense next generation method for constructing it.

To face-off with the entrenched, heavily subsidized modern foreign-flag fleet of over 200 ships, operating on American shores free of U.S. corporate taxes and without having to hire American crews or abide by America's "rules of the road" in terms of immigration and workplace compliance, an American operator has to have a competitive 21st century build plan and a highly differentiated product. It doesn't take a Harvard MBA to know that anything less than that — anything conventional in size or concept — will simply not make the grade.

There is no way to legislate around a bad plan, an uncompetitive product or an uncompetitive production methodology. That is exactly what MARAD and the Congress did with respect to the American Classic Voyages' "Project America" — a most regrettable chapter in American pork and politics.

Staying the Course

"Don't argue about the difficulties. The difficulties will argue for themselves." —Winston Churchill

As a result of the American Classic Voyages' debacle, Congress and the Administration turned a blind eye to Title XI and the prospects for an American flag cruise ship industry. It has taken years, but finally the story has faded from Congressional memory and the pressing need for job creation and economic growth has taken the forefront.

Most Members of Congress who were familiar with the "Project America" fiasco, except perhaps Senator John McCain, have moved on or forgotten. Senator McCain had long held that Title XI was a "subsidy" or "corporate welfare" and that, if a project is economically sound, Title XI wouldn't be needed. World City argued that the Senator's assumption was based on the premise that an economically sound project, regardless of its scale and scope, even a start-up, could be *commercially* financed. That isn't the case and this was confirmed by a number of prominent investment bankers and lending institutions.

This is all the more so in today's economy where the commercial lending environment has changed dramatically and investors are wary. The important elements in using Title XI, or any other government loan guarantee program, are economic soundness and risk management. Both of these elements are well documented in World City's Title XI Application and both were lacking in that of American Classic Voyages.

Senator McCain has always been a major supporter of the American Merchant Marine and of the U.S. shipbuilding and tourism industries. It is optimistically expected, based on current economic realities, that when political support is next needed for the American Flagship project, it will be forthcoming from the new administration and both sides of the aisle.

Knut and World City America Inc. believe that it is again possible to rebuild the momentum which had been mustered for the American Flagship project. Over $55 million has been invested in the city-ship project and Knut is convinced that the project will succeed if World City America Inc. stays the course. His theory is this. If you have a great idea whose business viability has been proven out in the industry and that not only makes good common sense, good business sense and promises great returns to all the stakeholders, not just the shareholders, you cannot lose. Just weather the storms, stay the course, and don't give up.

When pigs fly

What is truly amazing about the foreign-dominated cruise industry is the manner in which it has so consistently emulated the ideas and innovations that Knut and Tage Wandborg introduced with the city-ship project without giving them or World City any credit for the ideas, at least publicly.

On the contrary, some in the industry have been outspokenly critical of just about every innovation and new idea that Knut and Tage introduced, be it the ever-increasing size of cruise ships, the wisdom of shorter cruises and closer-to-home itineraries, broadening the markets to be served, and the concept of offering guests the added space, amenities, programs, entertainment and activities that have become standard in the industry, albeit not yet on the same scale as the city-ship project.

> They copied all they could follow
> but they couldn't copy my mind
> so I left them sweating and stealing
> a year and a half behind.
>
> Rudyard Kipling
> *(1865-1936)*

As an example of the industry's scoffing to the press, while steadily, if incrementally, incorporating Knut's and Tage's great ideas in their newbuild projects, Carnival's Bob Dickinson was once asked about the prospects for the American Flagship Project.

"When pigs fly," he proclaimed.

Knut's response to that was to quote Winston Churchill on the subject of America's *can-do* spirit: "The national psychology [of

Americans] is such that the bigger the Idea, the more wholeheartedly and obstinately do they throw themselves into making it a success. It's an admirable characteristic."

When Ted Arison, Carnival's late Chairman and Knut's former agent, was asked by the press what he thought about the size of Kloster's announced city-ship project, he chose his words carefully to add an element of fear: "The passengers will be lost at sea," he said. Nonetheless, as Kloster predicted, ships have gotten bigger and bigger, including Carnival's ships; not for bigness itself, but in order to bring together, on one hull, more opportunities for excitement, personal enrichment and entertainment which guests are increasingly coming to expect of a cruise vacation.

Imitation is the best form of flattery – or is it?

Several cruise lines, including Carnival and Royal Caribbean, have used World City's phrase "city-at-sea" to describe some of their larger cruise ships — even before Royal Caribbean International (RCI) introduced its 220,000 gross registered ton Genesis class ship currently under construction in Turku, Finland. But the use of the "city-at-sea" expression, in the context of sheer size, misses the whole point. For Knut, the "world city" concept has less to do with size and more to do with soul, spirit, animation, culture, sense of community and sense of purpose.

RCI's Genesis comes much closer to the city-ship's 255,000 gross registered tons and is basically double the size of most of the cruise ships competing in the market today. When introducing the project to the media, there was no mention of its forerunner or that many of the innovations, and certainly the entire concept

In Turku, Finland, John Rogers and Dick Baumler (left) and Admiral Kime and Tage Wandborg (right) pose with Finnish shipyard executives during the yard's design review.

of "ship as destination" and "city-at-sea", were originated in Knut's Phoenix project.

The shipyard in Finland that is soon to deliver the first Genesis class vessel, had, at the curious suggestion (read "requirement") of the United States Maritime Administration (MARAD), reviewed the World City design from top to bottom a few years back. It was the then Acting Maritime Administrator who indicated to Admiral Kime, World City's Senior Technical Advisor, that MARAD would not approve World City's Title XI application unless an experienced foreign yard reviewed the design and gave it its blessing (even though the design had been thoroughly reviewed and accepted by the United States Coast Guard and America Bureau of Shipping). The Finnish yard was "suggested."

In World City's good faith effort to comply with MARAD's seemingly endless, non-statutory and wholly discretionary added "requirements," World City America Inc. paid a sizable fee to the Finnish yard for its "detailed review" and "blessing." The design was given an A+ and the then Acting Maritime Administrator coincidentally landed a top job at a U.S. shipyard which had the same owner as the Finnish yard at that time.

Now, a few years later, much of World City's multi-million dollar design and engineering package and many of its programmatic aspects have resurfaced at that yard as Royal Caribbean's "revolutionary" Genesis class ship, including costly engineering features developed to comply with safety and evacuation requirements, design concepts such as World City's "town squares" and themed "neighborhoods," right down to World City's cantilevered aircraft carrier main deck and innovative lifesaving craft.

"It's OK," says Knut, "It proves the viability of the concept that the industry scoffed at for years. I wish them well." That's Knut.

Tage Wandborg, the ship's architect, Dick Baumler, the project's marine engineer, Helen Bentley, the first signer of the Build America Caucus, and many others, were not so forgiving of the yard's unattributed use of many of World City's ideas and innovations.

Good friends and long-time collaborators, Tage and Knut.

Although Knut was twenty years ahead of the times — in ideas, innovations, practices and principles — he is not necessarily seen as a "prophet in his own land." He says he doesn't care about recognition. All he wants is for his fellow cruise executives to join him in thinking of ways to help the industry grow, to make it more socially and environmentally responsible, and to spread its benefits across the broad spectrum of stakeholders.

CHAPTER SIX
Listening to Gaia

Gaia* is the name given by the ancient Greeks to their goddess of Earth and is the root of words such as geography and geology. The Greeks looked at Gaia as a living being, the cultural equivalent of Mother Earth or Mother Nature. In modern times, this "living Earth" idea resonates with new meaning.

The Gaia Theory, developed by the renowned British scientist James Lovelock, proposes that the air, the oceans, the rocks, and all living organisms on Earth evolved together as a single, inseparable system. This system serves to keep our planet in balance and habitable. According to the Gaian theory, the Earth regulates itself, much the way our bodies unconsciously maintain temperature, heart rate and other vital functions.

Many scientists, environmentalists and spiritual leaders have embraced the Gaia Theory because it evokes a great sense of belonging to and caring for our natural world. The idea of Gaia gives us a better understanding of our planet's strengths and frailties by emphasizing that humankind and the Earth's resources are inextricably linked. It helps put our environmental concerns in a new perspective by approaching the Earth's ills in much the same

*Pronounced guy-yah

way we approach illness and disease in our bodies, through prevention, treatment and cure.

GAIA the Viking ship

When he first learned of Jim Lovelock's work on the Gaia Theory, Knut immediately embraced the concept. At that time, he was co-sponsoring with the Norwegian Broadcasting Corporation and the governments of Iceland and Norway, a millennial celebration of Leif Eiriksson's[11] voyage to America, called "Vinland Revisited." To reenact the voyage, Knut acquired an exact replica of a one thousand-year old Gogstad Viking ship, described as "a poem carved in wood." She would be named *GAIA*, after Mother Earth. The name had been suggested by Iceland's then President, Vigdis Finnbogadottir, and Knut readily endorsed the idea. "By choosing that name," he said, "we are giving the voyage the right profile.

Former President of Iceland, Vigdis Finnbogadottir, christens the Viking ship, GAIA.

[11]This is the Norwegian spelling of the name.

Our mission simply is to create a better understanding of what Gaia (Mother Earth) is all about, and what needs to be done to take care of her."

Knut supported the Vinland Revisited project because, in his own words:

> It touches the spirit of exploration and discovery, the basic sense of having to stake something, in the pursuit of important goals. The willingness to take risks. Simple as that. And that's a spirit we need more than ever in the world today, with the tremendous environmental challenges with which we are faced, and the deepening gap between the rich and poor in our common present.

The purpose of the Viking ship voyage was clearly expressed in the Icelandic/Norwegian Vinland Revisited Agreement: "Our primary aim is to gain respect for the environment of which we are only a part. After 1,000 years of discoveries, we still have not learned to live

GAIA passes a huge iceberg on her way to Greenland.

in harmony with the planet and each other. We have yet to discover our common future."

When interviewed on the subject, Knut added that he also was supporting the project "because I am fond of my country and proud of our history as a seafaring people. From the early Viking voyages to our modern fishing and shipping industries, the ocean has always been our best friend and — sometimes — worst enemy. That's how it is in Iceland, too. We truly have common roots going far back in our history and deep into the ocean."

GAIA sailed from Norway to Iceland, Greenland, Newfoundland, Boston, New York and, finally, Washington, D.C.

GAIA's "map" for the voyage was the "Declaration for a New Global Agenda" prepared by Worldwatch Institute whose mission is to "deliver the insights and ideas that empower decision makers to create an environmentally sustainable society that meets human needs." (www.worldwatch.org)

Worldwatch Institute focuses on 21st century challenges including climate change, resource degradation, population growth and poverty. Knut found the Worldwatch declaration thought-provoking and an appropriate mission for *GAIA's* voyage. It states, for example, that "the goal of the cold war was to get others to change their values and behavior, but winning the battle to save the planet depends on changing our own values and behavior."

In a speech he gave at the MIT Club of Boston upon *GAIA's* arrival there, Knut explained why he viewed the Worldwatch declaration as such an appropriate "map" for the Viking ship's mission:

> Over the course of history our European forefathers have extended their dominance over new continents, cultures and natural resources. The discovery of America, the subjugation of the old Indian cultures, the slave trade and the colonization

Upon GAIA's arrival in New York, there was a ceremony at the South Street Seaport Museum. Seen here, left of podium, is Hon. Gro Harlem Brundtland, Knut at the podium and GAIA's Captain, Ragnar Thorseth, to the right.

of the rest of the world were all stages in this expansion. While our wealth and technology ended mass poverty among our own people, others had to pay with their cultural traditions and their natural resources. Those of us who reaped the benefits of our forefathers' expansion are 60 times wealthier than the poorest of the lands we conquered.

Today, we no longer have a new continent to which we can expand and no more civilizations to exploit. Still, expansion and economic growth continue to be the mainstay of our society — and now it is the environment itself that is made to suffer.

Knut Utstein Kloster, September 16, 1991, MIT Club Boston

The Worldwatch declaration stands for the proposition that the long term improvement in the human condition is contingent upon substituting environmental sustainability for growth as the overriding goal of national economic policymaking and

international development. An appropriate "map" and mission for
GAIA's voyage.

When *GAIA* reached a port of call, her huge sail was lowered and,
in its place, a large banner was raised. It read:

> **A Thousand Years Ago**...Europe and America were brought
> together by the Vikings.
> **Since then**...Our knowledge of the world has grown faster
> than our sense to take care of it.
> **Now**...we must set the right course ahead and open up a
> new era.

A roundtable discussion entitled "From Vinland to Mars: The
Legacies of Explorations" was scheduled for the end of the voyage
and to be held at the Smithsonian Air and Space Museum
in Washington, D.C. With a thousand years of discoveries behind

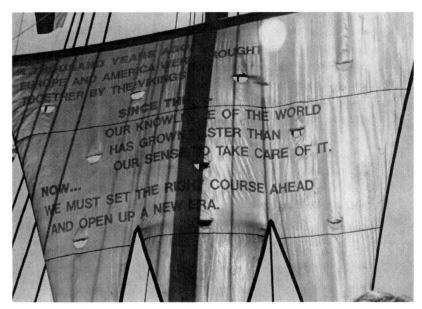

GAIA's mission banner

us, from the early Viking voyages through Columbus and other great seafarers, to our modern voyages in space, the conference was intended to query what past discoveries tell us about the course we must follow in the future to meet the environment and development challenges of our time.

When the Vinland Revisited journey ended in Washington, D.C., Knut was asked: "Did we make it?" His answer:

> Well, Ragnar Thorseth, the ship's Captain, and his crew — and *GAIA* — certainly did! The voyage was indeed a risky venture in spite of all the modern equipment on board, but they took the risk and made it.
>
> What about the rest of us? The Norwegian Government, the Icelandic Government, the Norwegian Broadcasting Corporation, and World City Discovery — the four partners

Norwegian Prime Minister, Hon. Gro Harlem Brundtland, watches with pride as Kloster congratulates GAIA's captain, Ragnar Thorseth.

who signed the Vinland Revisited Agreement and its "Declaration of Purpose," did we make it?

From the point of view of commemorating Leif Eiriksson and the voyages of a thousand years ago, Vinland Revisited was undoubtedly a great success. Many people were involved and they deserve our heartfelt appreciation.

However, taking our declared purpose seriously — as we should — we must ask ourselves: To what extent did we accomplish the task of actually showing how important it is that the spirit of discovery in our modern times be aimed at shaping our common future?

This, of course, is a question to which there cannot be given a clear cut answer. But I think it is fair to say that in her special way, *GAIA* has touched the minds and hearts of thousands of people. If all of us use the memory of Vinland Revisited to re-shape our values and behavior, then we will have made it, too.

GAIA to Rio and the Earth Summit

Preparing for the Smithsonian conference, Knut began to think about how the Viking ship *GAIA* might serve a larger purpose than that for which she was initially commissioned. He was thinking a great deal about the upcoming United Nations Conference on Environment and Development (UNCED – "Earth Summit") planned for Rio de Janeiro in June of 1992. Working with John Rogers and the World City team in New York, and with Maurice Strong, the Secretary-General of the Conference, it was decided that, after Washington, *GAIA* would set her course for Rio. En route, she would gather thousands of messages of hope and concern from the world's children and young people and deliver those messages to world leaders attending the Earth Summit.

These were exhilarating times. To prepare for *GAIA's* voyage to Rio, contact was made with the then Executive Director of UNICEF, James R. Grant. It was decided that *GAIA* would sail to Rio under a UNICEF banner: KEEP THE PROMISE FOR A BETTER WORLD FOR ALL CHILDREN. The theme was anchored in the World Declaration and Plan of Action from the World Summit for Children which had been held a year earlier at the UN.

Upon *GAIA's* arrival in New York, her new UNICEF banner was raised in a jubilant ceremony on the East River, outside the UN headquarters. Children from the UN School gathered along the pier to show their support, and about fifteen of the students came on board the *SPIRIT OF NEW YORK*, which its owners had kindly donated for the ceremony, to participate in the celebration. The children read their own messages addressed to world leaders about their concern for the future of the planet and their own futures. A number of fire boats sprayed a shower of blessings on *GAIA* as she set sail for Washington, D.C., and then Rio de Janeiro and the 1992 Earth Summit.

In Washington, *GAIA* was greeted by dignitaries including

Viking ship GAIA departs with her message of hope from United Nations Headquarters in New York.

101

Norway's Queen Sonja, and Iceland's President, Vigdis Finnbogadottir, await GAIA's arrival in Washington, D.C.

President G.H.W. Bush went aboard GAIA with two of his grandchildren to welcome GAIA to the nation's capitol.

Norway's Queen Sonja, Iceland's President Vigdis Finnbogadottir, and the U.S. President, George H.W. Bush. Hundreds of school children gathered to give their messages to *GAIA's* crew, and sang "We Are The World," as the Viking ship came into view.

After Washington, *GAIA* sailed to Port Canaveral where Jim Lovelock (founder of the Gaia Theory) and Apollo Astronaut, Jim Lovell, addressed the spirited crowd

Disney characters, Donald Duck, Mickey Mouse, and Chip and Dale, join World City America Inc.'s Chairman and CEO, John S. Rogers, at Port Canaveral to bid GAIA a safe voyage to Rio.

British scientist, James Lovelock, on board GAIA at Port Canaveral.

Grade school children visit GAIA en route to Rio.

of hundreds as they gathered to bid *GAIA* farewell and fair seas on her journey to Rio.

From Port Canaveral, *GAIA* sailed to Cuba, Mexico, Dominican Republic, Puerto Rico, Jamaica, Antigua, Guadeloupe, Martinique,

St. Lucia, Trinidad, Venezuela, Guyana, Surinam and Manaus, the capitol city of the State of Amazonas in Brazil. Along her route, she gathered thousands of messages from children and young people for delivery by *GAIA's* crew to world leaders at the Earth Summit.

Gaia Camp in Amazonas

In cooperation with AFS Intercultural Program, Knut's Oslo-based World City Discovery brought together 150 students, aged 14-18 and representing 43 countries, to Gaia Camp Amazonas '92. The camp idea grew out of the wish to demonstrate how common concerns can be translated into positive action and also out of the wish to leave something behind of lasting value to commemorate *GAIA's* visit to the Amazon region.

The Amazon rainforest has come to stand as a prominent example of the dire global consequences that can result when development takes place at the expense of the environment. Brazilians have often had to bear the brunt of international criticism because of what is seen as a lackluster record in rainforest management. It was not surprising, therefore, that the City of Manaus, deep in the Amazon rainforest region, embraced the idea of Gaia Camp Amazonas '92: a piece of unimproved city property of 28 hectares would be transformed into a public park with nature trails and paths for the citizens of Manaus and visitors to the region to enjoy. The area would also serve as a "living laboratory," a rainforest microcosm, for school children and visitors to learn about animal and plant species indigenous to the region.

The initial planning and layout work for the park was done by volunteers from E.A.R.T.H., a program of the University of Costa Rica which is dedicated to teaching responsible natural resource management in the humid tropical regions of Latin America. The students' work at the camp was coordinated by local ecologists.

The students spent three weeks clearing away brush and trash, constructing paths and trails, and building steps, bridges and resting areas in the former wilderness, now named "Gaia Park." Signs were constructed which identified the flora and fauna that could be seen along the various trails. After a hard day's work at Gaia Park, campers returned to home base in Manaus where they participated in training seminars and discussion groups which focused on children, environment and development. Special emphasis was placed on the United Nations' *World Declaration on the Protection, Survival and Development of Children, and Plan of Action* for its implementation.

The idea at the heart of the camp, Knut said, "was that students be given the information and training necessary to translate their environmental concerns into concrete action upon return to their home communities."

Gaia Camp "ambassadors" cheer as GAIA departs from Manaus for Rio and the Earth Summit.

The Norwegian Prime Minister, Hon. Gro Harlem Brundtland, visited Gaia Park and planted a tree to commemorate the park's opening, which drew 2,000 visitors.

"The experience of these young people, living and working together for a common goal, made a deep impression on them," Knut said, "as illustrated by this excerpt from a statement written by one of the campers":

> During these days, I have sensed a deep unity, created by the unique mixture of so many cultures, backgrounds and personalities. Our main goal must be to revive our fundamental ability to love and appreciate the Earth, not only as the source of all material resources, but also for our psychological well-being.

During the last two days of camp, the students, who called themselves "Gaia Ambassadors," drafted their own messages of hope and concern about the environment and the future of the planet, to be carried by *GAIA's* crew to Rio and the Earth Summit. Six of the campers, representing six continents, joined *GAIA* for the last leg of the voyage from Manaus to Rio.

GAIALOGUE and Gaiafilm

BBC taped *GAIA's* exciting and challenging voyage from Norway to Washington and produced a video which aired on public television in Norway, Iceland, England and the United States. Since BBC's coverage ended in Washington, Knut put together an international film crew to cover the remainder of the *GAIA's* voyage. The end result was a spectacular and very moving film that was aired at the opening of the plenary session of the Earth Summit. With permission from the artists, the film featured the music of, among others, Lionel Richie and the late Michael Jackson ("We Are The World") and Bette Midler ("From a Distance").

Knut also arranged the publication and broad distribution of a journal, *GAIALOGUE*, to report on *GAIA's* activities and share photographs of the Viking ship's arrival in various ports-of-call and the festivities surrounding the visit. World City Discovery sent people ahead of *GAIA* so that school children could prepare their messages and local communities could organize educational and cultural events to take full advantage of *GAIA's* visit. Importantly, each issue of the *GAIALOGUE* had a *'Listening to Gaia'* article written by a prominent member of the world community. For example, Thor Heyerdahl, the noted explorer, wrote, in part:

> The message that *GAIA* carries from port to port — from the old world to the new, from the arctic world to the tropics — is a non-political, or rather pan-political call for the protection of the natural environment, for peace, and for political and economic justice for the future generations of the whole world. In a vessel designed in ancient times with elegant lines that could harmonize and cooperate with the ocean waves, *GAIA* symbolically seeks to leap forward in time and leave behind a millennium of barbarism and wars, building a bridge to a 21st century of harmony and cooperation among young people with sound minds in sound bodies, in a sound environment.
>
> We know that the indigenous inhabitants of the Americas lived in harmony with the forests, rivers, and mountains, and worshipped them. They had lived off the riches of the land and the waters for thousands and thousands of years before the first Europeans arrived in the Americas. Today we face

the extraordinary challenge of reconciling the complexities and benefits of an industrial civilization with the inescapable requirement that we, too, must learn to live in harmony with Gaia and to responsibly manage the resources upon which this civilization depends. If we listen carefully, Mother Earth will tell us about the right path to the new world we wish to discover.

Norway's Prime Minister, Hon. Gro Harlem Brundtland, who had served as Chairman of the UN World Commission on Environment and Development, wrote one of the '*Listening to Gaia*' articles for the *GAIALOGUE*. Here are some excerpts:

Our generation is gradually realizing something fundamentally new. The environment and development crisis will eventually affect us all, regardless of where we live and how affluent we seem to be...

Growing awareness and growing self-interest can produce the political momentum for the changes needed. Poverty is where we must really start. To combat poverty, we need growth — particularly in the developing countries. We need a new kind of growth that is not based on overexploitation of natural resources. Sustainable development as defined by the World Commission on Environment and Development is a key concept for a new kind of growth. Democracy and public participation are essential for sustainable development. Consciousness raising and public participation are key prerequisites for global change...

Our foremost responsibility to future generations is to ensure that there will be a world worth living in. The future generations are knocking on our door. The living conditions of our children and grandchildren will be determined now..."

Another '*Listening to Gaia*' article was written by Stephan Schmidheiny who, at the time, was the Chairman of the Business Council

GAIALOGUE
GAIA TO RIO

Number 7, April 30, 1992

GAIA to Rio...
a voyage of discovery
in pursuit of a new era...

to encourage
environmental responsibility
and equitable economic
development...

to learn how to live in
harmony with the earth...

to insure a healthier,
safer, and more secure
future in every
country in the world

Sailing Plan
One Month to Rio

Gaia Park Dedicated in Manaus by Norwegian Prime Minister

March 18, 1992, was a special day for the people of Manaus, a city of 1.5 million citizens, located deep in the Amazon rainforest. That was the day Prime Minister Gro Harlem Brundtland of Norway arrived to formally open the Gaia Park. There she planted the first tree in what marked the beginning of an international reforestation relay. Brundtland is the chairman of the World Commission on Environment and Development, and considered by many an unofficial global minister for the environment.

It may seem odd to choose to plant trees in Manaus, which is already so rich in natural forest. But the Brazilian rainforest is under siege. It is being cut down at an alarming rate, and reforestation is necessary.

The Gaia Park is located in a jungle-like forest region of 27 hectares within the Manaus city limits. The area has long been eyed by developers who would like to make use of the property for housing and other projects. But instead of another development, Manaus will now have a public park, a sanctuary for all to enjoy. The area also will be a microcosm of the rainforest and a 'living laboratory' for school children and visitors to learn about animal and plant species indigenous to the region.

Manaus

Recife

Rio

Prime Minister Gro Harlem Brundtland at Gaia Park tree planting ceremony.

This issue of GAIALOGUE featured the dedication of Gaia Park by Norway's Prime Minister, Hon. Gro Harlem Brundtland.

on Sustainable Development.[12] The Council was comprised of corporate leaders from around the world. In the years leading up to the 1992 Earth Summit, Mr. Schmidheiny was appointed by UNCED Secretary-General, Maurice Strong, to advise on business and industry. He called together 47 other chief executives who ran large companies such as DuPont, Volkswagon, Mitsubishi, Shell and Dow. The objective was to prove that environmental measures can be compatible with economic vitality. In 1992, the Council published *Changing Course: A Global Business Perspective on Development and the Earth* (MIT Press), a 350-page report which was published in seven languages and provided an outline for sustainable development and a survey of the myriad ways industry and environmental interests mesh. In his *GAIALOGUE* article, referring to the *Changing Course* report, guest columnist Stephan Schmidheiny wrote:

> I do not mean to suggest for a moment that we have all the answers or agreed on every word. But we were able to agree on directions. For example:

> A free, open market best suits sustainable development because it maximizes innovation and equity of opportunity and can produce the economic growth needed to fund environmental management. But this market must be made to reflect environmental as well as economic truths. The price of a product or service must reflect the cost of either cleaning up or preventing the damage associated with that product or service...

---

[12] As of this writing, Mr. Schmidheiny is Honorary Chairman of the successor organization, the World Business Council for Sustainable Development. The WBCSD gathers more than 170 of the most important global companies as members united by a common vision of sustainable development, based on three pillars: economic development, environmental balance and social progress. The council sets out to promote business leadership as a catalyzer for change towards sustainable development, based on eco-efficiency, innovation, and corporate social responsibility (www.wbcsd. org).

Just as there must be open markets nationally, so should there be internationally. Poor nations need to trade in order to develop, and need to develop in order to manage their environmental resources...

We had a lot to say to companies about using resources more effectively, preventing pollution, recycling, and setting up long-term commercial partnerships to transfer clean technology from those who have it to those who need it. We agreed on many other directions in which governments and companies might move, knowing we have to monitor progress and adjust the course along the way. Uncertainty as to destination must not prevent us from setting out.

But we also agreed companies that move along the lines of sustainable development are not only serving the needs of future generations, they are best serving the needs of their own stockholders and employees... the most eco-efficient companies will become the most valuable on the world's capital markets.

GAIA's arrival in Rio marks the official opening of the Earth Summit and Global Forum

It was the culmination of a 12-month, 15,000 mile voyage. *GAIA* emerged out of a hot maze in Baia de Guanabara off Flamengo Beach in Rio de Janeiro against the dramatic backdrop of Sugar Loaf Mountain. Her arrival was the main attraction at the opening ceremony of '92 Global Forum, the gathering of non-government organizations devoted to environment and development which took place simultaneously with the Earth Summit. Thousands of people who had come from every corner of the world to participate in the Global Forum and Rio Conference were on the beach watching as

GAIA arrives in Rio after her 12-month, 15,000 mile voyage.

GAIA slowly approached. Never before had a Viking ship visited these shores, and the excitement was palpable. Forget police barriers, never mind the waves and wet shoes, everyone wanted to witness this historic landfall.

GAIA's Captain, Ragnar Thorseth, made his way ashore in the ship's zodiac in the company of the six Gaia Ambassadors, carrying dozens of mailbags containing thousands of messages gathered by *GAIA* on her long journey. The messages were addressed to world leaders attending Earth Summit and meant to serve as a reminder to "keep the promise" they had made two years before at the UN World Summit for Children.

A large stage had been set up on the beach and a group of distinguished guests were on hand. Hon. Gro Harlem Brundtland, Prime Minister of Norway; Mario Soares, President of Portugal; José

Goldemberg, Environmental Minister of Brazil; Maurice Strong, UNCED Secretary-General; and Dr. Richard Jolly, Deputy Executive Director of UNICEF, to name a few. Actor Roger Moore, in his role as UNICEF spokesperson, hosted the ceremony. Knut was also present; his pride could not be contained.

As Ragnar Thorseth and his Gaia Ambassadors began making their way through the crowd to deliver their messages, spectators, reporters and photographers crowded around the speakers' platform in a media frenzy. Speeches, song and dance lasted until long after sunset — a fitting opening to one of the most important conferences of the century.

Gaiaday

It was June 2, 1992, a Tuesday. In his statement, welcoming *GAIA* to Rio and the Earth Summit, Knut made the following observations:

> When the Viking ship *GAIA* set her sail in Norway a year ago, she embarked on a long voyage that would finally bring her to the Earth Summit here in Rio. The purpose of it was simply to make a statement about our concern for the future. The world is like a big ship going in a dangerous direction. She now needs all the help she can get to move the rudder — and change the course — before it's too late.
>
> During the voyage, *GAIA* has been in touch with thousands of people in many countries. She arrives in Rio now with a cargo of messages to the world leaders, from children and young people. "Keep the promise," they say, "for a better world for all children."
>
> If all these messages could be translated into an agenda for world leaders, we would probably get close to what is

proposed in the *Human Development Report 1992*, recently published for the United Nations Development Program...

That report reminds us that the gap between rich and poor nations has doubled during the past three decades. Restricted and unequal access to the world's financial, trade and labor markets cost developing nations and their poor populations $500 billion annually. That is nearly ten times what those countries receive in foreign aid...

We who live in the rich nations must now understand that a fundamental improvement in the human condition worldwide is the key to a sound, environmentally safe future for our children and grandchildren.

A serious message, to be sure. That was, after all, the reason that over 30,000 people and leaders from every nation gathered in Rio for the Earth Summit and Global Forum.

But the festive spirit of the occasion also called for Knut to end his remarks on a lighter note. He suggested to the crowd that to constantly remind ourselves of the needs of Mother Nature and our responsibilities to her, we should name a day of the week in her honor. Since it was a Tuesday, the day of the week named after Tiw, a God of War, Knut suggested that Tuesday should be renamed Gaiaday and, as he stepped aside for the next speaker, he wished the crowd "Happy Gaiaday!"

Although Knut recognized that it wouldn't be easy to convince nations to change their calendars to rename one day of the week in honor of Mother Earth, he was (and remains) determined to promote the concept. To push the merits of his idea, Knut and his team had prepared two Gaiaday calendars, one for "grown-ups," to be distributed to world leaders at the Summit and corporate leaders around the world, and one for kids, to be distributed to schools and youth organizations.

The kids' version depicted some of the thousands of messages from children that had been gathered in communities along *GAIA's* 15,000 mile journey. The kids' calendar was named "Keep the Promise," and consisted of drawings, paintings, letters, and poems. On each page, there was also an appropriate quote from a world leader. For example:

> We must all seize this unique opportunity to advance the peace and happiness of mankind by translating into concrete actions the political will that has been so evident during preparations for this Summit.
>
> *President Moussa Traoré, the Republic of Mali*

and

> The Nicaraguan people are determined to strengthen peace so that our children will be able to take their rightful place in the future.
>
> *President Violeta Barrios de Chamorro, Nicaragua*

The "Keep the Promise" Gaiaday calendar was widely distributed during the Earth Summit and also sent to schools of the children who had visited *GAIA* along her 15,000 mile journey. The "grown-up" Gaiaday calendar was named *"Changing Course"* in honor of the forward thinkers who participated in the Business Council for Sustainable Development (BCSD) and helped to write their important report bearing the same title. In addition to stunning photographs of *GAIA's* historic and purposeful voyage, the *"Changing Course"* Gaiaday calendar featured quotes from the BCSD report and gave monthly examples of what global companies were doing to manage sustainable resource use and change in business and global partnerships. The Gaiaday calendar is a call to action, urging that a new course be set, one filled with promise for humanity and the Earth. Thousands of these calendars were distributed at Rio and sent to major corporate and business leaders around the world following the Summit.[13]

Mission Accomplished: Children's Messages Delivered to World Leaders

From the canyons of Manhattan they came; from sprawling cities and tiny coastal villages up and down the Atlantic Coast; from tropical islands in the Caribbean to the humid rainforests of Amazonas. In paints, crayons and calligraphy; as books and posters, poems and models. There were thousands and thousands of them brought to the shoreline by children and young people who visited *GAIA* on her 15,000 mile journey to Rio and the Earth Summit.

They were messages of hope and concern about our common planet, our common future. Flying her UNICEF "Keep the Promise" banner, *GAIA* would act as messenger of the young; her mission was to assure that their messages be delivered to the world leaders gathering in Rio for the Earth Summit.

On June 14, 1992, *GAIA* kept her promise. At the opening

---

[13] Erling S. Lorentzen, a founding Member of the Business Council for Sustainable Development, and then Chairman of Aracruz Celulose, an environmentally responsible Brazilian paper pulp manufacturer, contributed to the cost of the Changing Course Gaiaday calendar and arranged for its distribution to world leaders attending the Summit.

UN Secretary-General Boutros Boutros-Ghali and UNCED Secretary-General Maurice Strong applaud the children's presentation of messages to Brazil's (then) President Collor.

ceremony of the Plenary Session on the final day of the Earth Summit, following an introduction by Conference Secretary-General, Maurice Strong, and the showing of the video on *GAIA's* year-long voyage, two young *GAIA* ambassadors of all the world's children mounted the dais and presented arms full of messages to President Fernando Collor of Brazil. President Collor received the messages most warmly and attentively on behalf of more than 100 heads of state who attended the historic summit.

Knut spent millions of dollars on the *GAIA* to Rio project — a voyage of discovery in a new era. Why? In his own words, "to encourage environmental responsibility and equitable economic development; to teach young people that it is possible to live in harmony with the Earth; to ensure a healthier, safer and more secure future for every child in the world; and to harness the energy, spirit and commitment of young people everywhere."

Maurice Strong, Secretary-General of the Conference, wrote the final 'Listening to Gaia' column in the July 7, 1992 *GAIALOGUE*. Here are some excerpts from it:

The growing awareness of the need for sustainable development is, of course, inextricably linked with the unprecedented political, economic and technological changes that are transforming our world into a single, interdependent planetary society. This interdependence is marked by the increasing globalization of the economy and the global and systemic nature of environmental problems. It comes at a time when the frontiers between East and West are fading, but the gap between rich and poor is widening.

The gross imbalances that have been created by the concentration of economic growth in the industrialized countries and population growth in the developing countries, are at the center of the current dilemma. Redressing these imbalances will be key to the future security of our planet in environmental and economic as well as traditional security terms. This will require fundamental changes in both our economic behavior and our international relations. Effecting these changes peacefully and cooperatively is, without doubt, the principal challenge of our time.

The industrialized countries must take the lead in effecting this transformation, for the unparalleled economic growth that has produced their wealth and power has also given rise to most of the major global environmental risks we face. Developing countries share these risks but are only at the early stages of the economic development to which they aspire, and their right to grow cannot be denied. But their growth will clearly add immensely to global environmental pressures and risks unless they, too, can make the transition to more sustainable modes of development. They can neither afford nor be expected to do this unless they have access to the additional financial resources and technologies they require to integrate the environmental dimension into their development. Agreements on measures to meet these needs reached at the Earth Summit provide a promising starting point.
Of special importance is a massive attack on the vicious circle of poverty in which so many millions of people are caught

up, driving them to meet their immediate survival needs by destroying the environmental and resource base on which their future survival and well-being depends…

No one meeting, even such an historic gathering as the Earth Summit, with over 100 Heads of State in attendance, could be expected to make all the changes necessary. But the Earth Summit has, I am confident, established the foundations for a wholly new global partnership based on common and shared responsibilities, one in which developing countries will have the incentive and the means to cooperate fully in protecting the global environment while meeting their needs and aspirations for economic growth.

It would be easy to get frustrated and lose hope, particularly when we see with what difficulty genuine change is fraught, but Knut doesn't see it that way. He is convinced that every journey begins with a single step, that every light lights the way, and that the 30,000 participants who gathered at Rio for the Global Forum and Earth Summit — as well as the thousands of children who entrusted their messages to *GAIA*, and the thousands more who were inspired by *GAIA's* mission — have not forgotten what is at stake or that they have personal and collective responsibility to implement the changes needed to build a better world for all children. "Each of us must follow our own heart," he says, "I feel good about my *GAIA* investments. To me, Tuesday will always be Gaiaday, in honor of Mother Earth."

CHAPTER SEVEN
Planet Earth at Ground Zero

T he soul-shattering destruction of the twin towers at the World Trade Center in New York on September 11, 2001, was heard and felt in every corner of the world, and will never be forgotten.

When Knut learned that the Lower Manhattan Development Corporation (LMDC) was organized to assist New York City in recovering from the terrorist attacks and ensuring the emergence of Lower Manhattan as a strong and vibrant community, he wished to contribute in some meaningful way. He knew that the centerpiece of the program was to create a permanent Memorial remembering and honoring the thousands of innocent men, women and children lost in the terrorist attacks.

In 2002, the LMDC announced a design competition for a memorial that would honor the victims and recognize the endurance of those who survived, as well as the courage of those who risked their lives to save others:

> May the lives remembered, the deeds recognized, and the spirit reawakened be eternal beacons which reaffirm respect for life, strengthen our resolve to preserve freedom, and inspire an end to hatred, ignorance and intolerance.

Knut was very moved by the challenge and discussed with Tage Wandborg possible concepts for a fitting memorial at Ground Zero. Knut felt the importance of bringing the world together in this time of terrible loss and fear. He wanted to show the interdependence of peoples and nations and solidarity. He envisioned a huge globe as the centerpiece of the memorial, because it would remind everyone that Planet Earth, like the twin towers, is vulnerable and that each of us, and every nation, must come together in search of peace, justice and equality for all.

Tage wholeheartedly embraced the concept of the Globe — of Planet Earth at Ground Zero — and designed it as a breathtaking 750-foot wide big blue marble, reminiscent of the view of Earth from outer space, a precious and fragile jewel reflecting the sea and the sky. At night, the globe would be illuminated and appear as a sparkling diamond from miles around and from outer space. Inside Tage's huge globe was a 70-story atrium giving way on all sides to a rose sculpture in honor of the victims. It was proposed that the globe would stand on six elevator towers and float 150-feet above a beautiful memorial plaza, without touching the footprints of the twin towers.

Knut's idea for the Ground Zero Memorial, and Tage's design, were intended to provoke the sentiment of Adlai E. Stevenson in this excerpt from a speech to the UN Economic and Social Council, Geneva, Switzerland (9 July 1965):

> "We travel together, passengers on a little spaceship,
> dependent on its vulnerable reserves of air and soil, all
> committed, for our safety, to its security and peace.
> Preserved from annihilation only by the care, the work and
> the love we give our fragile craft." — *Adlai E. Stevenson*

Due to the economic downturn, the plans of the Port Authority of New York and New Jersey to rebuild at the site have been put on hold. It's possible that Knut's idea for a memorial, and Tage's design, may still come to be, if not at Ground Zero, then on the high seas (see Author's Note).

CHAPTER EIGHT
Creative Capitalism

Bill Gates uses the term "creative capitalism" to describe the notion that profit and social responsibility are not mutually exclusive and that capitalism can also improve the lives of those who have not traditionally benefited from modern market forces — such as the billion people on the planet who live on less than a dollar a day and do not have basic necessities such as access to clean water and electricity.

In an article written for *Time Magazine* (August, 2008), Gates describes creative capitalism as "an attempt to stretch the reach of market forces so that more companies can benefit from doing work that makes more people better off." The article is supplemented with a number of excellent examples, such as Grameen Bank in Bangladesh which has disbursed more than $7 billion to over four million of the world's poor, of which 94% are women (98% of the loans have been repaid — a recovery rate higher than any other banking system); Sumitomo Chemical which shared technology with a Tanzanian textile company that has made millions of insecticide-treated mosquito nets (mosquito nets are crucial tools in the fight to eradicate malaria); and Vodaphone which bought a large stake in a cell phone company in Kenya that has found ways to serve the economic needs of low-income Kenyans and make a profit doing it.

Time Magazine also conducted a roundtable discussion on creative capitalism. John Mackey, founder and CEO of Whole Foods, was among the panelists. He prefers to use the phrase "conscious capitalism" — what he describes as a 21st century business paradigm that embraces the complex interdependencies of the multiple constituencies involved. This, in essence, is what Knut has been advocating for the past three decades. The interdependency and interconnectedness of all the stakeholders is the reality in which corporations exist today and, according to Mackey, "our economic and business theories need to evolve to reflect this truth."

Mackey says that the common perception about the purpose of business — i.e., to maximize profits — is a myth. "Most entrepreneurs do not start the businesses in order to maximize profits." Referring to Bill Gates, Mackey said: "He had a passion for software; he wanted to put computers everywhere, he wanted to transform the world. That was the passion... that's not about maximizing profits, but it worked pretty well!"

Mackey argues that a transformation is needed in the way we think about business. "People want businesses to do good in the world. It's that simple." Conscious capitalism, as John Mackey sees it, and practices it, is a new social/political/economical/environmental business model which encourages the entrepreneurial spirit for good:

> In my business experience, profits are best achieved
> by not making them the primary goal of the business.
> Rather, long-term profits are the result of having a deeper
> business purpose, great products, customer satisfaction,
> employee happiness, excellent suppliers, community
> and environmental responsibility — these are the keys to

maximizing long-term profits. The paradox of profits is that, like happiness, they are best achieved by not aiming directly for them.

(http://www.flowidealism.org/Downloads/JM-CC-1.pdf)

Economist Milton Friedman who wrote that "there is one and only one social responsibility of business — to use its resources and engage in activities designed to increase profits so long as it stays within the rules of the game, which is to say, engages in open and free competition, without deception or fraud." Like Knut, John Mackey disagrees. They, and many other enlightened leaders, believe that corporations should try to create value for all their constituencies. "From an investor's perspective," Mackey argues, "the purpose of the business is to maximize profits. But that's not the purpose of the other stakeholders — for customers, employees, suppliers and the community. Each of those groups will define the purpose of the business in terms of its own needs and desires, and each perspective is valid and legitimate." Mackey's business model is one that "more consciously works for the common good."

That model is the one that Knut has embraced in his businesses for many decades. It is encouraging that successful business people, such as Bill Gates and John Mackey, have helped put this topic on people's radar screens, and, most importantly, that they are putting their money and brains to work on the potential of capitalism to make the world a better place and spread the benefits of the free market system.

In 1987, Knut gave a speech at the International Association of Independent Tanker Owners (INTERTANKO) annual meeting. Intertanko is a group of independent tanker owners who have as their goal to "ensure that the oil that keeps the world turning is shipped safely, responsibly and competitively."

In his speech, Knut said that he had been motivated to accept the invitation to speak, in part, by the fact that "no specific theme" for the speech had been suggested. He interpreted that to mean he could "talk freely" about what he sees as "perhaps the most fundamental of all our mutual interests today [i.e.] to promote free enterprise and create new business opportunities for the maritime industry by participating actively in the process of moving the world forward in the right direction."

Many of the things Knut said in that speech track the message Bill Gates gave in his *Time Magazine* article and in his January 2008 speech at the World Economic Forum, as well as John Mackey's public statements about "tapping into more powerful motivations than self-interest alone." Here are some relevant excerpts from Knut's 1987 speech:

> Our objectives as companies and as an industry should clearly continue to be as result-oriented as before in terms of bottom line profitability and return on invested capital. But our visions of the future must be expanded in scope. ***

> No longer would it be adequate to say that our job is just to transport cargo from A to B. A new dimension would be added in our traditional evaluation of profitability. This kind of thinking is the way to position the whole maritime industry in the large, global picture. It results in strategies which are right, which strengthen the image of "free enterprise" as a constructive and socially responsible force — and it gives us the opportunity to play an active part in shaping and, in the long run, gaining lasting benefit from — a well-balanced, equitable and sustainable economic growth worldwide, with international trade and transportation as the basis for our existence. ***

> The shipping industry is, by nature and tradition, the most internationally-oriented industry in the world. Now is the

time when we should put ourselves in the driver's seat and place the concept of "free enterprise" in a value system which will be perceived by people everywhere — through our attitudes, actions and the way we conduct ourselves — as being good and meaningful. ***

The task now is to define our global mission and set a new course which will strengthen our basis for making money and for meeting other objectives as well. From what I have said here already it will not come as a shocking surprise to you if I suggest that the maritime industry should take the high road and let its agenda focus on the role we could play as a major visionary pathfinder in the world. For example, at the next INTERTANKO Annual Meeting it would be interesting to generate a well-prepared discussion on what the trend in supply and demand for tankers would be if an industry course is set for a more equitable distribution of energy in the world, as conceptually defined in the report from the UN Commission on Energy and Development. Or take the Law of the Sea — as a gateway to opportunities in undersea mining and farming which could generate new technical, transportation and other services. Or the United Nations Environmental Program (UNEP) with "Earthwatch" and the possibility of making our ships active participants in the process of protecting the environment. ***

Great rewards in the way of new commercial opportunities could be gained by expanding our vision, our horizon, and our commitment to larger goals.

An article in the Norwegian paper *Dagens Næringsliv* in the early 1990's dubbed Knut the "Kind-hearted Capitalist." Again, we see his forward-looking recognition that business has a role beyond profit-making:

It is plain to see that Knut Utstein Kloster travels off the beaten track…everyone agrees that Kloster is a man of contradictions, a genuine combination of capitalist and idealist, a wealthy and influential businessman who is deeply concerned with the deplorable state of the world — and who truly wants to do something about it. ***

He sighs deeply and gazes out the window. The view is wide and lovely from the offices of World City Corporation in Ullern Alle. From here Kloster directs a number of activities which he hopes will wed his concern for environmental and developmental issues to conducting business in a sensible way. ***

Make no mistake, Kloster is still a businessman with blind belief in the power of the market economy. "The role of the market is to identify demands and fulfill them. But is it up to the politicians to determine the parameters? I believe the business community must play a far more active role. Meanwhile, we must devise a more meaningful way to measure real growth in our society: A concept such as the gross national product makes no sense because it doesn't include the future cost of today's pollution and depletion of resources. We need some sort of awakening — something that will foster a new awareness and new attitudes." ***

Is Knut Utstein Kloster a giant Pooh Bear, a merchant of milk and honey with the seven seas as his Hundred Yard Forest? Or is he a man ahead of his time, a prototype for the humane and socially enlightened leader of the future?

The "awakening" and "new attitudes" to which Knut was referring are seen today in leaders like Gates, Mackey, Google founders Sergey Brin and Larry Page and many others. Fortunately for the planet and for the free market system, there are many more such visionaries and socially responsible entrepreneurs today than when Knut was being labeled a "naïve dreamer" for having such thoughts and convictions back in the 60's, 70's, 80's and even in the 90's.

The Role of Conscience

In 1991, the *Boston Globe* wrote an article about Knut, calling him "the conscientious capitalist" and "one of Europe's most successful proponents and defenders of free enterprise." The article quotes Knut as saying that free enterprisers are "going to have to promote new values that start taking care of Mother Earth."

> Kloster doesn't claim to know the way out, nor does he see himself as the environmental crusader who will rally the forces. He maintains he's just a small addition to a burgeoning group of capitalists with a conscience.

Capitalism with a conscience is also described as "social entrepreneurship," the practice of seeing profit-making as only one element of success, with the company's impact on customers, employees, the community and the environment as the other determiners of "success." It's clear to Knut that conscience plays a big role in how capitalism will be defined by the global community in the years to come.

In dictionaries, conscience is defined as 1. "the sense of what is right or wrong in one's conduct or motives, impelling one toward right action;" and 2. "the complex of ethical and moral principles that controls or inhibits the actions or thoughts of an individual."

In a homily defending the "The Rights of Conscience" given in 1995 in his homeland of Poland, the late Pope John Paul II described conscience as "man's most secret core, and his sanctuary." Deep within our conscience, he explains, we discover a law which we have not laid upon ourselves but which we must obey.

Our conscience is our inner guide, our "true north," and it also is our judge. Pope John Paul II reminded us that "to be a person of conscience means… working for what is good… it means courageously assuming responsibility for public affairs... being concerned for the common good and not closing our eyes to the misery and needs of our neighbor..."

Conscientious capitalism, then, is capitalism that integrates economic, social, environmental and other criteria; it considers such issues as climate change strategies, energy consumption, human resources development, knowledge management, technology sharing, stakeholder relations and transparency and accountability in corporate governance.

Knut Utstein Kloster has, throughout his life, exemplified this caliber of corporate and global citizenship. He has "walked the talk" for decades — long before it became a popular subject which, still today, is more talk than walk for far too many corporations and corporate leaders.

In a speech that he gave to the Norwegian-American Chamber of Commerce in 1981, Knut spoke about "The challenge and conscience of a capitalist in today's society." I'm going to share much of that speech with you because I think it touches the heart and goes to the core of the subject:

> Since we have just finished an excellent meal, let's start with a story about a prominent Senator from Oregon who hosted a luncheon for his colleagues. At the plate which was served, his — I presume — somewhat startled guests around the table found just a tiny piece of meat and a very small potato, nothing else. In his welcoming speech the Senator told them that the purpose of serving such a meager meal was simply to show them — or remind them of — how much food the great majority of people in the world got every day to sustain their lives. I don't know if he also mentioned the fact that about 80,000 children die every day from starvation or malnutrition.
>
> The message here of course — in the context of our theme today — is clear: Since everything is relative in this world,

each and every one of us being here today at the Waldorf Astoria is a super privileged capitalist as compared to the mother and the father of the child who is dying right now... and now... and now — every second, day in and day out, all year round. The clock is ticking off the painful hours, and deep down in the abstract part of our conscience we all feel guilty about it.

As a business man, however, I am not supposed to regard this catastrophe as particularly relevant to what I am doing. My job is defined in terms of commercial activities, not in terms of saving the world and the children who are dying. That is for the politicians to do. That's their work. They have been elected to deal with it — to solve all the big problems — poverty, starvation, violence, unemployment, the arms race, energy shortage, pollution — you name it. Thank God we have the politicians! ***

Whenever people in the U.S. are polled on their attitudes toward institutions in the country, business ranks close to the bottom. It's no use moving backwards into the future, but if we talk about the multinational companies' impact on the world, it is difficult to push under the carpet the fact that the whole free enterprise concept in a global perspective very often is associated historically with exploitation and so-called "economic imperialism." Rightly or wrongly. And we are all in the same rich-country boat here, whether we like it or not.

Therefore, if we want the world to be a friendly open market for our products and services in the future, we must in my judgment challenge ourselves continuously — ideologically, philosophically and morally. We must define the nature of our business in terms and in a language which is understood and accepted, and we must conduct ourselves and our operations in a manner which can be respected widely.

For example: What do we mean by "free" enterprise? Perhaps we should begin to talk more about a *sound* enterprise system or a *healthy* enterprise system, because it can be free without being very healthy, but it cannot be healthy without a reasonable degree of freedom. It is like talking about *life* standard instead of living standard. You can have a good living standard without a good life standard, but you cannot have a good life standard without a reasonably good living standard.

When it comes to our goals and business objectives, it is not adequate any more to just say that the name of the game is profit or to make money even when we talk about it off the record. Yes, we must have a reasonable financial return on the invested capital — that goes without saying — but what is capital? Money? Yes, but that is only part of it.

In his new bestseller, *The Third Wave*, Alvin Toffler has a chapter on "The Corporate Identity Crisis" where he talks about the "many bottom lines," or multiple bottom lines — social, environmental, informational, political and ethical bottom lines — all of them interconnected. He also talks about the concept of social reporting and the new language of accountability. Indeed, he says, accounting itself is on the edge of revolution and is about to explode out of its narrow economic terms of reference.

The Shell companies for example today list five overall corporate goals — only one of which is to achieve a "reasonable return on investment" — and specifically states that each of the five goals, economic and non-economic, must "carry the same weight" in corporate decision-making. The goal accounting method forces the companies to make their trans-economic objectives explicit, to specify time periods for their attainment, and to open this up to public review. ***

The notion that you have to do well financially before you can do so-called "good" is fundamentally misleading. But it is a difficult process indeed for many reasons to implement effectively such goals — partly because they tend to challenge our deep-rooted, traditional attitudes.

In such a perspective it seems logical to say that a capitalist is someone who is in a position to decide how money, human resources and influence are being used for a common purpose. ***

As business leaders we should begin to move ourselves more freely into the mainstream of society, and not just stay in our traditional boxes, in the same old conservative place, with low personal profiles so that nobody can see us. If the business community is suffering from a credibility gap in society, or if it is difficult for us to communicate our ideological message effectively — one of the reasons perhaps is that we are perceived by society to be rather faceless and impersonal, conservative and reactionary, and not really to be trusted because of our narrow preoccupation with the task of making money. ***

Essentially the aim here is to transfer development capacity from the rich countries to the poor — to stabilize raw material prices — and open up markets in the rich countries for goods produced in the poor countries. I believe that if the chairman and/or chief executive officers of the 100 biggest corporations in the world today came together up in the Norwegian mountains or on a small Pacific island somewhere, they would find a way to reach the unreachable star: A master plan for helping the politicians save the world and all the children who are dying. Nothing more, nothing less! ***

Many small brooks make a big river, as we say in Norway, and the opposite of love is not hate but indifference. Life is like a tug-of-war — between ambitions and compassion, facts and feelings, heads and hearts, winners and losers, dreams and so-called realities. I think it was Robert Kennedy who said that "some people see things as they are and ask WHY — I dream of things that never were and ask WHY NOT?"

It hurts the flickering soul. Thank you.
Norwegian-American Chamber of Commerce, New York,
September 30, 1981

Thankfully, Knut's vision about the 100 biggest corporations getting together up in the mountains to tackle the world's biggest problems, is now happening each year at the World Economic Forum (WEF) in Davos, Switzerland — thanks to the shared vision of Professor Klaus Schwab and the many international corporations and other organizations that support the forum.

Progress is being made and the more examples we have and models to follow, the sooner creative capitalism will be able, to use Bill Gates' expression, "take wing," or, to use Mackey's expression, "reach the take-off point."

Throughout his career, like most other leaders, Knut has faced challenges that called upon his conscience, his inner compass, to steer a course that he believes to be right but which may or may not be "popular."

Conscience must guide every aspect of one's life and work. In the business arena, the goal must be to achieve commercial success in ways that honor ethical values and respect people, communities and the environment. Although intangible assets, such as leadership, innovation, vision, creativity, willingness to take risks, corporate social responsibility, etc., are not measured, nor often even reported in corporate financial statements, these assets are every bit as important as physical and financial assets in terms of creating value and long-term wealth. In the "owner-entrepreneurial" model of capitalism, the interests of the owner and shareholder are aligned. But in the era of institutionalized ownership, intangible assets — like a corporate conscience and a deeper sense of purpose — can be lost.

Knut's entrepreneurial ventures provide stunning examples of how value is created through intangibles such as vision, courage, conviction, risk-taking, conscience and compassion. One intangible which is not seen very often in the capital markets today is patience. Yes, patience. In today's world, there is much too much emphasis on short-term performance, rather than long-term value creation. It is a worrisome trend, to be sure. Long-term wealth creation — such as human capital, technology, innovation, supplier alliances, environmental performance, reputation and brand — are often sacrificed on the altar of near-term profit maximization.

All too often institutional and speculative investors are detached from the businesses in which they have invested. They are "owners" but they don't act like owners; they act like speculators. The result is that management is diverted from achieving the company's strategic objectives, competitiveness is weakened and investments in research and development as well as in environmental performance are sacrificed to meet quarterly earnings expectations. Instead of a partnership of interests organized to create wealth, many corporations are being bought and sold like real estate. John Sunderland, Chairman of Cadbury Schweppes, is quoted in a *Financial Times* article, *The Short-Term Shareholders Changing the Face of Capitalism (3-28-06),* as saying:

> I may be old-fashioned but I view a shareholder as a shareholder — someone whose interests in the success and prospects of the company last more than three weeks... I have real concerns about promoting the use of my company's stock as hedge fund plays — just as I would if they were chips in a casino.

Every industry has the opportunity now to reinvent itself in ways that address the world's difficult social, economic and environmental problems. In each case, it will be a matter of conscience — using our businesses to make money, yes, but also steering a course toward a more just and equitable global economy and a healthier Planet Earth. So whether you call it creative capitalism or conscious capitalism or conscientious capitalism or just corporate social responsibility, it all adds up to doing the right thing and for the right reasons. In this, Knut Utstein Kloster has been an exemplar.

"Kind-hearted Capitalist"

CHAPTER NINE
Green Clean Global Village®

K nut's wonderful and exciting vision of a 21st century hospitality product ("city-at-sea") that can follow peak seasons and good weather and bring together the best civilization has to offer in terms of recreation, education, culture and personal enrichment — while contributing meaningfully to our common quest for a better future — is nonetheless short of perfect. It is not a zero emission vessel.

There are no commercially available technologies that will permit the vessel to sail without releasing some emissions into the atmosphere. The city-ship will be powered by GE gas turbines which have the lowest possible impact on the environment, including invisible smoke at any power, lower emissions than traditional marine diesel engines, low particulates, no heavy fuel sludge by-product, and utilizing cleaner burning marine gas oil. A special Selective Catalytic Reduction system (SCR) is installed on the exhaust of the turbine, suppressing NOX and CO. In addition, there will be a flue cleaning system of scrubbers incorporated into the ship's funnels which further cleans the exhaust before it enters the atmosphere.

Knut and World City America Inc. have weighed the pros and cons of introducing the prototype city-ship, as it is described above and in further detail in Chapters Four and Five, even though it will contribute to marine pollution, albeit on the lowest scale possible.

On the *pro* side, the ship is as green as it can be and will consume the lowest amount of fuel per passenger of any ship in the world. It will utilize solar, wind and wave energy to the maximum extent practical, and it will sail at slow speeds most of the time, which reduces emissions. Since the ship is the destination, long voyages are not contemplated, and coastwise itineraries are planned so that the ship can be accessed by over a 100 million passengers who are within an hour of a point of embarkation, be it by automobile, bus or train. This is a huge fuel savings in terms of air travel normally associated with a cruise vacation. And most importantly, the operation of the ship will be making money for World City Foundation and its larger goals, including global environment and development initiatives. Moreover, the ship itself will be used as a global forum for important international events and activities and be conducting classes, seminars and lectures designed to educate and inform guests and meeting attendees on ways in which they can personally, professionally and organizationally contribute to the search for solutions to our common environmental, societal and economic challenges.

Pending the availability of commercial technologies, such as small modular atomic engines that will enable the city-ship to operate as a zero emission vessel, a decision has been taken to continue with the existing design, but with the engine and fuel storage capacities reconfigured so that, when such technology is approved for commercial use, it can be added without a major conversion. In the interim, Knut is supporting World City America's ongoing campaign to create a zero emission ship that can serve as an example and demonstrate that shipping and marine pollution need not be synonymous.

Biosphere at Risk

While many climate experts were, for a time, generally in agreement that global warming is a serious threat to the planet, some climatologists now question the trend and even warn of a new "Little Ice Age."[14] While the dynamics of climate change are complex and subject to differing theories as to cause and effect, civilization cannot ignore the possibility that a buildup of greenhouse gases could, in the century ahead, destabilize the entire biosphere, causing sea levels to rise, creating extreme temperatures, violent storms, devastating droughts, the spread of disease, and the destruction of food production and human habitability in many areas of the globe.

Knut has correctly observed that "The public doesn't know what to believe, but we all understand that oil is a precious resource that our generation should not be squandering, and we all understand that CO_2[15] emissions are polluting our air, damaging our health and that of future generations."

Sailing smokestacks

Global shipping is responsible for a very substantial part of total carbon dioxide (CO_2) emissions. The United States Congressional Research Service (CRS) reported in 2008 that there were over 46,000 commercial vessels sailing the seven seas, including tankers, bulk carriers, container ships, barges and passenger ships.

[14] *The Economist,* September 27, 2008, citing, e.g., Dr. Philip Stott, Emeritus professor of biogeography, University of London.

[15] CO_2 (carbon dioxide) - a colorless, odorless, non-combustible greenhouse gas that is formed by complete combustion of fossil fuels and carbon-containing products; it also is released through respiration by living organisms and by the gradual oxidation of organic matter in soil. CO_2 is generally believed to contribute to global warming. BusinessDictionary.com

The air pollution is generated by diesel engines that burn high sulfur content fuel, producing sulfur dioxide, nitrogen oxide and particulate matter, in addition to carbon monoxide, carbon dioxide and hydrocarbons. Most commercial ships rely on residual fuel oil, also called "bunker fuel," which is a tar-like sludge left over from the refining of petroleum. Bunker fuel is cheap, less than two-thirds the rate of marine gas oil, according to a report in the *Wall Street Journal*.[16] Cruise ship operators do not use bunker fuel; they use an ultra-low sulfur diesel fuel (ULSD), which has a much lesser impact on the environment. World City has chosen to specify gas turbines which use an even cleaner burning marine gas oil. Nonetheless, the impact of commercial shipping on the environment is extremely serious and Knut has decided that he might be able to use his reputation and experience as a shipping executive to advance public awareness of and technical solutions to the marine pollution problem. Except for ports and coastal regions, marine pollution often escapes notice, which is how and why the problem has grown to such seemingly unmanageable proportions.

The above-referenced *Wall Street Journal* report claims that "Ships release more sulfur dioxide, a sooty pollutant associated with acid rain, than all the world's cars, trucks and buses combined," citing a recent study by the International Council on Clean Transportation.[17]

The referenced *Wall Street Journal* article continues to cite the ICCT study stating that "ships produced an estimated 27% of the world's smog-causing nitrogen-oxide emissions in 2005. Only six countries in the world emitted more greenhouse gases than were

---

[16] Ships Draw Fire for Rising Role in Air Pollution, by Bruce Stanley, November 27, 2007.

[17] The International Council on Clean Transportation (ICCT) was formed in 2001 for the purpose of improving the environmental performance of cars, trucks, buses and transportation systems in order to protect and improve public health, the environment and quality of life. www.theicct.org

produced collectively in 2001 by all ships larger than 100 tons, according to the study and United Nations statistics." (The ICCT study entitled *"Air Pollution and Greenhouse Gas Emissions from Ocean-going Ships"* can be found on ICCT's website: http"//www. theicct.org/documents/48_06_ICCT_OceanReportComplete_04-4_ taiwanRe).

As Knut observed, even if it is ultimately determined that CO_2 is not a cause of global warming or that global warming is not being caused by human activity, there are other threats from increased atmospheric concentrations of CO_2. Ocean acidification, which occurs when CO_2 in the atmosphere reacts with water to create carbonic acid, has already increased ocean acidity by 30 percent according to Woods Hole Senior Scientist Scott Doney, who specializes in marine biogeochemistry and ecosystem dynamics and is considered an expert on the global carbon cycle. The full effect of ocean acidification on marine ecosystems and organisms that inhabit them are not yet known, but scientists and policymakers are concerned.

According to Doney, ocean acidification leads to wholesale shifts in seawater carbonate chemistry and will severely impact many organisms that build shells from calcium carbonate (e.g., corals, algae, plankton) by the end of this century. Doney believes that changes in the water cycle and ocean circulation will likely decrease the ability of the land biosphere and oceans to store carbon and that the resulting carbon-climate feedbacks could impact climate change. (*"The Dangers of ocean acidification," Scientific American,* 294 [3], March, 2006, 58-65.)

Although much research remains to be done in this area, the trend of ocean acidification is understandably disconcerting when considering the devastating consequences that acid rain had on freshwater ecosystems during the last century. "Acidification impacts on processes so fundamental to the overall structure and function of marine ecosystems that any significant changes could have far-reaching consequences for the oceans of the future and the millions of people that depend on its food and other resources for their livelihoods," reports Doney.[18] Scientists believe that the combination of warming, rising sea levels, pollution, overfishing and acidification threaten to disrupt the ocean's well-balanced chemical and biological processes. Reducing carbon dioxide emissions will be critical to minimizing these threats. Ocean currents circulate the energy and water that regulate our climate and weather, affecting every part of the human experience.

Oceana, a not-for-profit organization that campaigns to protect and restore the world's oceans, published a comprehensive report which takes the position that the shipping industry is responsible for a significant portion of the climate change problem and of ocean acidification (www.oceana.org/shipping-impacts).

The global shipping industry is virtually unregulated, although the International Maritime Organization (IMO), a specialized agency of the United Nations, was created to develop and maintain a comprehensive regulatory framework for shipping, including safety, environmental concerns, technical cooperation and maritime security. The IMO was established to adopt legislation, but individual member governments are charged with implementing those regulations. The problem, of course, is that some countries lack the experience, expertise and resources necessary to do this properly. Others "put enforcement fairly low down on their list of priorities," the IMO concedes.

The IMO International Convention for the Prevention of Pollution from Ships affirms the right of a coastal state to take

---

[18] *The Annual Review of Marine Science,* March 2009, 1:169-92

measures to protect their coastline and, in the United States, California and Alaska have passed laws to regulate emissions and other marine pollution. The UK and Baltic States have also enacted legislation to protect their coastal regions.

In 1990, the IMO passed the International Convention on Oil Pollution Preparedness, Response and Cooperation (OPRC), which provides a global framework for international cooperation in regulating and preventing marine pollution, but it operates on a consensus basis. Despite the IMO's good intentions, it is clear that the problems are bigger than the mechanisms in place for dealing with them.

Greenhouse gas emissions from ships are not currently regulated by the United States government or limited under the Kyoto Protocol or other international treaties that address global warming. Pressure is mounting and environmental and other citizen groups are taking action into their own hands. In July of 2008, for example, a coalition of conservation groups and state attorneys general threatened to sue the U.S. Environmental Protection Agency for its failure to address global warming pollution from ocean-going ships. Earthjustice, an environmental law firm that is handling the matter, estimates that a single ship coming into harbor can generate the smog-forming emissions of 350,000 new cars. Ship exhaust has been linked to respiratory illness, cancer, heart disease and premature death, Earthjustice said.

California has passed a law that requires ships within 24 miles of its coastline to burn low sulfur fuel in their auxiliary engines. Los Angeles and Long Beach, the nation's two largest container ports, are encouraging ships to approach ports at slower speeds, which will reduce emissions, and they have provided facilities whereby ships can turn off their engines and receive their power from ashore.

"For a long time," Knut said, "people assumed that the oceans were big enough to cope with any pollution caused by human activity, but we now know this is not the case." The oceans cover over 70 percent of the globe and it is the Earth's largest and most important ecosystem. It controls our climate and the primary source of protein for a billion people around the world. "As one of the leading sources of carbon dioxide emissions and other greenhouse gases, the shipping industry has a huge responsibility, as do all other sectors of the global economy, to embrace solutions that will start to reverse the damage," Knut said in a recent interview.

Global shipping activity has increased by three percent per year for the last three decades and this rate of growth is projected to go up. Unless something is done to reduce the use of residual oil (bunker) and other steps taken which will reduce emissions and improve the efficiency of vessels, predications are that shipping pollution will double from 2002 levels by the year 2020 and triple those levels by 2030.

While cruise ships represent a small fraction of the entire shipping industry, they nonetheless can have a serious impact on the environment, depending on how the operator deals with wastes, including sewage, solid waste, graywater, ballast water and oily bilge water. Cruise ship emissions are cleaner than other types of ships, but they still contribute to the pollution of the air and water.

Call to Action – Green Clean Global Village®

As a pioneer in the shipping industry, Knut saw an opportunity to leverage his leadership, experience, and concern for the environment to spearhead a major movement in the maritime industry. The overall goal would be to dramatically reduce marine pollution and, at the same time, work to increase public awareness of the planet's environmental and energy problems and the role each of us can play in the search for solutions. Knowledge and information are great tools in the battle to engage public opinion and participation.

It became clear to Knut that the city-ship project — because of its revolutionary scale and anticipated visibility as one of the world's largest manmade floating structures — has the potential of playing an important role, as exemplar — not just for the burgeoning cruise sector but for the entire shipping industry. The goal is to create a zero-emission, wholly energy efficient, totally environmentally benign vessel. Such a ship could serve as an energy demonstration platform and an energy research center where new wind, solar and wave technologies are efficiently utilized as supplements to a main 100 MW(e) atomic engine which simultaneously produces hydrogen for the ship's fuel cells. "It's a simple concept, but difficult to implement," Knut said, "and for all the wrong reasons. There are a lot of misconceptions about nuclear energy in commercial applications. But," he added, "there is no way around it for the future of the planet. What I envision is a self-sustaining ship, or village, producing its own water, responsibly treating its own waste, and not generating any pollution — a Clean Green Global Village.®"

Knut's sea-going version of a Green Clean Global Village (GCGV) would also fill the city-ship's original mission by making money as a destination resort while serving as a global forum — welcoming thought-leaders, scientists, business executives, government officials, professors, teachers and concerned citizens. Our children and grandchildren would see that it is possible to enjoy 21st century amenities and pleasures without taxing the environment or future generations.

Terrestrial energy is the solution – it's sustainable, safe and green

In his new book, *Terrestrial Energy: How Nuclear Power Will Lead the Green Revolution and End America's Energy Odyssey*, veteran journalist William Tucker explains that nuclear energy is "terrestrial" — the same process that heats the center of the earth. Tucker points out that "every fuel used in human history... has been derived from the sun. But," he explained in a *Wall Street Journal* article (July 21, 2008), "terrestrial energy is different":

> Terrestrial energy is the heat at the earth's core that raises its temperature to 7,000 degrees Fahrenheit, hotter than the surface of the sun. Remarkably, this heat derives largely from a single source -- the radioactive breakdown of uranium and thorium. The energy released in the breakdown of these two elements is enough to melt iron, stoke volcanoes and float the earth's continents like giant barges on its molten core.

> Geothermal plants are a way of tapping this heat. They are generally located near fumaroles and geysers, where groundwater meets hot spots in the earth's crust. If we dig down far enough, however, we will encounter more than enough heat to boil water. Engineers are now talking about drilling down 10 miles (the deepest oil wells are only five miles) to tap this energy.

> Here's a better idea: Bring the source of this heat -- the uranium -- to the surface, put it in a carefully controlled environment, and accelerate its breakdown a bit to raise temperatures to around 700 degrees Fahrenheit, and use it to boil water. That's what we do in a nuclear reactor.

Tucker's use of the word "terrestrial" is accurate and helps remove the stigma associated with nuclear weaponry.

A year-long investigation into the pros and cons of "terrestrial" energy for the city-ship led Knut and World City America Inc. to conclude that it provided the only path to a zero-emission Green Clean Global Village® at sea and the only practical long-term solution to the marine pollution problem. The same conclusion has to be reached when searching for a clean, safe, reliable and competitive land-based energy source on a scale that is required. Only "terrestrial" energy can replace a significant part of the fossil fuels (coal, oil and gas) which massively pollute the atmosphere and contribute to the greenhouse gas effect.

The United States has over 100 nuclear reactors providing approximately 20% of the nation's energy. After twenty years of steady decline in the industry, several factors have fueled a resurgence. The United States government has now committed significant R & D funding with the objective of rebuilding the nation's leadership in nuclear technologies. Over the past two decades the industry has been working with the Nuclear Regulatory Commission (NRC) to certify a number of third generation advanced reactor designs. Several of these new designs were found by the NRC to dramatically exceed safety goals. The Energy Policy Act of 2005 provides many new incentives for the nuclear power industry including tax credits, risk insurance, loan guarantees and additional support for advanced nuclear technologies.

Research and Development on nuclear energy in the United States has taken place at a number of Department of Energy laboratories, particularly the Idaho National Engineering and Environmental Laboratory (INEEL, formerly INL), as well as at numerous universities. Focus is on advanced, next generation nuclear power systems for both electricity and hydrogen production. The goal is to develop a plant that will be smaller, safer, more flexible, and more cost-effective than any commercial nuclear plant in history and clear the way for the long-term future of the industry, as well as a way to replace imported oil with domestically produced, clean and economic hydrogen.

In February 2006, the U.S. government announced a Global Nuclear Energy Partnership (GNEP) whereby it "will work with other nations possessing advanced nuclear technologies to develop new proliferation-resistant technologies in order to produce more energy, reduce waste and minimize proliferation concerns." As part of this initiative, partner nations will develop a program whereby nuclear fuel is provided to developing nations which will allow them to enjoy the benefits of nuclear energy in exchange for agreeing to forego enrichment and reprocessing activities. This program will further alleviate proliferation concerns.

The World City technical team, led by Tage Wandborg, World City's naval architect, and Dick Baumler, its marine engineer, researched various near-term atomic energy technologies which might be suitable for marine application.

Terrestrial energy is a necessary component in addressing the energy crisis

Despite the continued existence of a highly vocal anti-nuclear movement, Knut and the World City team have been persuaded that atomic energy is one of the best solutions to environmental public health problems, as well as a necessary and probably central part of any effort to meet the world's increasing energy demands. "The benefits of nuclear energy are real; its problems are hypothetical," says Larry Foulke, past president of the American Nuclear Society and co-author of *Dispelling the Myths About Nuclear Power,* a brief prepared for the National Center for Policy Analysis:

> When decisions are made concerning future sources of electric power in the United States, facts, not fear, should be the basis for appraising the nuclear industry's place in the mix.

James Lovelock, creator of the Gaia Theory that Earth is a single self-regulating organism (see Chapter Six) was anti-nuclear for many years but he has now concluded that nuclear power is the last, best hope for averting what he calls "climatic catastrophe." It was Lovelock who encouraged Knut and World City to look into the possibility of atomic energy for the city-ship. According to Lovelock:

> Opposition to nuclear energy is based on irrational fear fed by Hollywood-style fiction, the green lobbies and the media... Even if they were right about its dangers — and they are not — its worldwide use as our main source of energy would pose an insignificant threat compared with the dangers of intolerable and lethal heat waves and sea levels rising to drown every coastal city of the world. We have no time to experiment with visionary energy sources; civilization is in imminent danger and has to use nuclear, the one safe, available energy source, now, or suffer the pain soon to be inflicted by our outraged planet.

Patrick Moore, one of the founders of Greenpeace and its Director for many years, has joined Lovelock and many other environmental activists in converting from anti-nuclear to pro-nuclear on the basis of solid scientific facts, as well as environmental realities.

Gwyneth Cravens has written an important book, *Power to Save the World: The Truth About Nuclear Energy,* in which she dispels decades of misinformation and misconceptions about nuclear energy. Cravens' comprehensive and compelling narrative debunks every argument that has been advanced by the anti-nuclear movement and forces the conclusion that nuclear energy is the only real solution to the world's increasing energy demands and the hazards associated with burning fossil fuels. Another valuable work on the subject is *The GeoPolitics of Energy: Achieving a Just and Sustainable Energy Distribution by 2040,* by Judith Wright and James Conca.

Since public perception — and misinformation — are the main obstacles to the so-called "nuclear renaissance" in this country, Knut asked his colleagues at World City America Inc. to suggest ways in which he and they could contribute to widening the debate and dispelling many of the myths and misunderstandings that surround this issue.

More than ever before, corporate leaders and individuals are stepping up and taking a stand on important issues such as the climate and energy crises. Knut saw the advantages of tapping into that encouraging movement and leveraging the potential benefits of his own public awareness campaign and the Green Clean Global Village® initiative.

Sergey Brin and Larry Page, Google's founders, have committed billions of dollars to helping to solve the world's "biggest, most imminent, and least well resourced problems," including global poverty, global health and sustainable development. As part of this ambitious agenda, Google is committed to helping build a "clean and green energy future."

Dr. Larry Brilliant — who takes after his name — was chosen as Google's "guru of giving" and made Executive Director of Google. org, the organization that will make grants and also investments to advance these goals. Dr. Brilliant has spent his life implementing large-scale solutions to big social problems such as eradicating smallpox and preventing millions of people in developing countries from going blind. He has also run large public companies, including tech firms. In the 60's, Brilliant was anti-corporate, but now he sees and believes that corporations can have a major role to play in solving the world's problems. Choosing Brilliant was obviously the right choice.

Google also is committed to using its enormous IT clout to advocate public policy that will "accelerate the development and deployment of cost-effective energy efficient and renewable energy technologies in order to achieve deep and rapid reductions in greenhouse gas emissions".

On the energy front, Google.org launched a multi-billion dollar strategic initiative whose mission is to develop electricity from renewable sources cheaper than electricity produced from coal (RE<C) and to do it in years, not decades. The announced focus is on solar thermal power, wind power technologies and enhanced geothermal systems.

Google Inc. and Google.org are among the most likely contacts for Knut and World City in advancing their own public awareness campaign about marine pollution and the role of nuclear energy in addressing it. Although none of Google's announcements ever touched the word "nuclear" or even "alternative" energy, it seemed clear to Knut and World City that nuclear energy would have an important, if not singular, role to play in each of Google.org's five "core initiatives." Three of these initiatives relate to fighting climate change. "Whatever position one takes on the role of humans in creating the crisis," says Kloster, "it is undisputed that reducing greenhouse gases is part of the solution, just as clean, reliable and affordable energy is the centerpiece for sustainable economic development," which happens to be Google's fourth "core" initiative.

The fifth initiative relates to global health and, particularly, developing an early warning system for pandemics and other disasters. Without electricity, any global health or development initiative will obviously be severely limited in its reach.

Jesse H. Ausubel, Director, Program for the Human Environment at The Rockefeller University (http://phe.rockefeller.edu/jesse/) was one of the main organizers of the first UN World Climate Conference in Geneva in 1979. He was also the main author of the 1983 report *Changing Climate* which was the first comprehensive analysis of the greenhouse effect. Ausubel considers himself a "heretic" among Greens. He argues that renewable sources of energy, such as solar and wind, are not green. "To reach a scale at which they would contribute importantly to meeting global energy demand, renewable sources of energy, such as wind, water and biomass, cause serious environmental harm."

> Cheerful self-delusion about new solar and renewables since 1970," says Ausubel, "has yet to produce a single quad of the more than 90 quadrillion BTU of total energy the U.S. now yearly consumes... Let's stop sanctifying false and minor gods... *Renewable and Nuclear Heresies, Int. J. Nuclear Governance, Economy and Ecology, Vol. 1, No. 3, 2007.*

According to Ausubel, technologies succeed when economics of scale are present — when the technologies grow smaller even as they become more powerful, like computer chips. In other words, if an energy system is to grow, it must shrink in size and cost. "Considered in watts per square metre," argues Ausubel, "nuclear has astronomical advantages over its competitors." However, if the nuclear industry is to meet its full potential, it must expand out of its niche market, i.e., providing baseload electricity, and start making hydrogen as well. Ausubel sees methane as the means for accomplishing this. (See "*The Future Market for the Energy Business,*" *APPEA Journal* 2007, Part 2 – 487-494)

One can't responsibly argue with Ausubel's science, or his numbers, but it's a free world and surely possible to say that "watts per square meter" of space isn't necessarily the *be all and end all* in comparing or choosing energy technologies to tackle the world's energy and climate problems. Nevertheless, Knut says it would be interesting to put Ausubel in the same room with Dr. Brilliant and Messrs. Page and Brin, as well as other energy experts, to explore the perceived (or misperceived) advantages of solar and wind technologies, which Ausubel insists simply *are not green* and will never generate a fraction of the planet's baseload electricity requirements:

> They may be renewable but calculating spatial density proves they are not green. The best way to understand the scale of destruction that hydro, biomass, wind and solar promise is to denominate each in watts/m2 that the source could produce. In a well-watered area like Ontario, Canada, 1 km2 produces enough hydroelectricity for about a dozen Canadians while severely damaging life in its rivers. A biomass power plant requires about 2,400 km2 of prime Iowa farmland to equal the output of a single 1,000 MW nuclear power plant on a few hectares. Windmills to equal the same nuclear plant cover about 800 km2 in a very favorable climate. Photovoltaics require less but still need a carpet of 150 km2 to match the nuclear plant. *** No economics of scale adhere to any of the solar and renewable sources, so trying to supply India or eastern China would require increases in infrastructure that would overwhelm these already crowded lands. Moreover, the photovoltaics raise nasty problems of hazardous materials. Wind farms irritate with low frequency noise and thumps, blight landscapes, and whack birds and bats. And solar

and renewables in every form require large and complex machinery to produce many megawatts. While a natural gas combined cycle plant uses 3.3 metric tons (mt) of steel and 27 m3 of concrete, a typical wind energy system requires construction inputs of 460 mt of steel and 870 m3 of concrete per average MW(e), about 130 and 30 times as much. Bridging the cloudy and dark as well as calm and gusty weather take storage batteries and their heavy metals. Burning crops inflates the price of food. Renewable energies also invoke high risks as sources of supply in a changing climate. Clouds may cover the deserts investors covered with photovoltaics. Rain may no longer fall where we built dams and planted biomass for fuel. The wind may no longer blow where we build windmills.*** Without vastly improved storage, the windmills and photovoltaics are supernumeraries for the coal, methane and uranium plants that operate reliably around the clock day after day. We live in an era of mass delusions about solar and other renewables, which will become an embarrassing collection of stranded assets. But let's use our intelligence and resources to build what will work on the large scale that matters for decarbonization rather than to fight irrationality. *Renewable and Nuclear Heresies, Int. J. Nuclear Governance, Economy and Ecology,* Vol. 1, No. 3, pp. 229-243, 2007.

World City's research, including reading the work of and often making contact with some of the nation's and world's most prominent organizations, scientists and environmentalists, as well as authors, government officials and corporate and business leaders in the energy field, led Knut to conclude that nuclear energy provides the only green solution to baseload (large scale) energy requirements, both here at home and in developing nations. Renewables such as wind and solar and geothermal, while worth pursuing for niche applications, could not begin to deliver energy on a scale that is required now, let alone in the decades to come and in places such as China and India where energy requirements are escalating at a phenomenal pace. There appears to be very little legitimate basis for disagreement with this proposition.

Nor can wind and solar even begin to provide the power requirements of World City's city-ship or the globe's expanding merchant fleet if it is to back away from residual oil and other fossil fuels that have such a devastating impact on the health of the environment and our oceans' complex ecosystem.

Knut's goal is simply to gather the best and the brightest brains on the energy issue and to meet with world business leaders, including Google's leadership, in the hope of enlisting their participation in the campaign to promote a science-based debate on nuclear energy, as well as to seek encouragement of the campaign to reform the shipping industry. Knut genuinely believes that his Green Clean Global Village® initiative is poised to play an important role in that challenge.

Tom Friedman, the Pulitzer Prize winning author and noted *New York Times* journalist, moderated a segment in January 2008 at Davos in which Google's founders and Dr. Brilliant discussed Google's ambitious energy initiatives. And Friedman was extremely convincing in an hour-long interview with Charlie Rose on how "green" is the "new red, white and blue." Although Friedman is a known supporter of nuclear energy, the word nuclear did not come up in the Davos session or in the Rose interview. Knut asked this author to write Friedman to ask him why and also to suggest that if business leaders, such as Messrs. Brin, Page, and Gates, agree to the brainstorming session that Friedman moderate it.

In his excellent book, *Hot, Flat, and Crowded: Why We Need a Green Revolution — and How It Can Renew America* (July 2008), Friedman spends a lot of time extolling renewables, such as wind and solar, with nuclear energy given a somewhat lesser presence, but the overall treatment of the subject — which places emphasis on energy conservation and energy efficiency — is a wake-up call to America and a tremendously convincing story about what is needed on the part of the government, industry and each of us to secure a leadership role in what he calls the coming "Energy-Climate Era."

Friedman uses the term "Code Green" — "making America the world's leader in innovating clean power and energy-efficient systems and inspiring an ethic of conservation toward the natural world." Code Green, says Friedman, "has to involve both a strategy for the generation of clean energy — in order to mitigate climate change and its effects on weather, temperatures, rainfall, sea levels and droughts — and a strategy for the preservation of the earth's biodiversity so we don't destroy the very plant and animal species that sustain life."

Knut's Green Clean Global Village® initiative and his effort to widen the debate on the important role of nuclear energy in solving both the energy and climate crisis, while campaigning to end marine pollution, is a potentially powerful response to Friedman's provocative Code Green call-to-action.

CHAPTER TEN
Friend of Man

"He was a friend to man, and he lived in a house by the side of the road."

— Homer

Not that long ago, it became universally incorrect to speak or write generically about man, men, mankind, as if women didn't exist. Knut took it to the extreme for a while by never failing, no matter how awkward the sentence, paragraph or speech would become, to add "/she" beside the word "he" or "/women" beside the word "men" or to change "mankind" to "humankind" in his writings and communications. That was in the 80's.

True, he comes from one of the few countries that, at that time (and still) fully recognizes the merits of women and often elects women to the nation's highest posts. Knut also has a beautiful, strong, well-educated, independently-thinking psychologist wife and two beautiful, strong, well-educated, independently-thinking daughters[19] so it all probably came easier to him than to most of us,

---

[19] I should add here that he also has two handsome, strong, well-educated, independently-minded sons.

in terms of daily use.

With advance apologies, then, for the use of the word "Man" in this chapter heading, it is taken from the Sam Walter Foss (1858-1911) poem "The House by the Side of the Road." The Homer quote above is also applicable to Knut's unassuming home by the side of the road in the outskirts of Oslo. Knut's home is different than what one would have expected, knowing of his social status going back two generations of a prominent Norwegian shipping family. The house is warm, comfortable and inviting but not large or extravagant in any respect. It fits neatly into the landscape and the neighborhood, right by the side of the road. Foss' poem captures how Knut sees himself and his place in the world:

> "Let me live in a house by the side of the road,
> Where the race of men go by—
> The men who are good and the men who are bad,
> As good and as bad as I.
> I would not sit in the scorner's seat,
> Or hurl the cynic's ban—
> Let me live by the side of the road
> And be a friend to man."

Knut truly is a friend of man in the universal (man / woman, haves / have nots) context. He has a heart of gold and it shines through every step he takes and every decision he makes.

Exitus acta probat — By their deeds ye shall know them

Knut seen here with Kahnin as a puppy.

Knut's "best" friend over the years has been his German Shepherd. In recent years, there has been Kahnin, Egon and Kelly.

Knut's love of animals and respect for nature has been the theme of his whole life. For example, he stood up against whaling in Norway where whaling is deeply rooted in the country's culture, economy and history, and where many fellow Norwegians, and the Norwegian government, support whaling, believing that it can be done in a responsible and sustainable manner. For Knut, it was a brutality issue:

> The whale is warm-blooded and feels pain just like human beings. Slowly dying after being harpooned is torture pure and simple. Biologists say that whales have a nervous system similar to our own and that the animal therefore experiences

pain and fear much the same way as we do. The harvesting
method is gruesome. Obviously, there are many other animals
that also suffer, but we are now on the subject of whales.
There is a relationship between how we treat animals and
how we treat each other as human beings.

Standing up for employees' rights is another example. As a shipping
executive, Knut always considered it a matter of conscience, as well
as good business, that the crews onboard his ships were treated with
respect and dignity, that they received fair wages and that they be
provided with decent accommodations and adequate facilities. "The
ships are the *home away from home* for the crew," he said. "This is
an ideological and also a pragmatic issue, because without a happy
crew, you cannot expect good service or proper maintenance of the
vessels." When Knut was at the helm of NCL, the Caribbean crews
were covered by a general agreement with the Norwegian Seaman's
union. No other cruise operator at that time, or for many years
thereafter, had the same reputation for the crew's welfare. There is
no question that Knut's good example gradually had an impact on
the industry and, today, most of the major cruise companies have
overhauled their policies and now at least provide decent minimal
accommodations for their crews on the newer, larger ships.

In the early 70's, Knut was a regular contributor to the prominent
Norwegian business magazine, *KAPITAL*. As in all aspects of his life,
he was never hesitant to speak up for what is right or to write about
subjects that go beyond straight *business* and make a broader point
or lesson or just show the human side of life. One article was entitled
Åpent hus, or "Open House." The article started with an anecdote:

> One evening some years ago a lot of demonstrators gathered
> outside an American Embassy. As usual, windows were
> smashed. Suddenly the lights went on, the door was opened,
> and out came the Ambassador himself. He invited the

demonstrators to come in. Coffee was served and politics was discussed. The lights were not turned off again until late into the night. Since then there has been little, if any, demonstration outside the Embassy.

At about that time, Knut explained, Finn Gustavsen, the late Norwegian socialist-politician had appeared on television and fired what Knut viewed as a very unfair and untruthful salvo at Norwegian shipowners. The shipping industry in Norway typically "laid low" and didn't comment on the Gustavsen attack. Knut felt that the better approach would be to come out, turn on the lights and invite the critic to openly debate the issues raised. This is what the "Open House" article was about. "I don't exactly believe that Finn Gustavsen would have eaten humble-pie, but maybe he would be a bit more careful when, the next time around (in spite of his knowledge), he expressed such opinions," Knut wrote.

In some of the articles, Knut talked about love, marriage and family. In this 1973 piece, he addressed the role of the husband/father:

> It is Saturday morning, quiet in the office and bad weather. In the paper I noted that Bishop Alex Johnson and Member of Parliament, Berit Ås, will talk about marriage and the family in the old celebration hall at the University starting at 10:15. Why not? So, a half an hour later I was sitting there, together with lots of women and a few men.

> "The foundation of marriage is love, and its purpose is happiness," a wise man said in 1799. And thus came into being the myth about marriage as a happiness automaton. *** No, marriage certainly is no happiness automaton, Alex Johnson said. It is a heavy load being pulled by two people together. *** Alex Johnson called the relationship between mother, father and child the "biological triangle," and he did not hide his optimism about the family institution despite all the gloomy predictions about its breaking up and destruction.

Marriage and family have a strong position in society, he said, and in his opinion they would prevail in the future. ***

Enter Berit Ås. She focused on the women's position in marriage and the family: To what extent today do married women with children experience the so-called "biological triangle" as a living social reality? She referred to findings showing that the father is together with his children only an average of 8 minutes every day (half an hour on Saturdays and Sundays). And then she noted all the other things that make the mothers' position so difficult, and her self-image so frail.

In reality, Berit Ås said, strong indications are that the family is one of the weakest institutions we have in society. It's only the man who is clinging to the myth about the family because he needs it as a resource. He is dependent upon having a woman behind him, who takes care of the unsalaried production which housework is. Talking about self-confidence and self-realization are empty phrases in the man's mouth, as long as he is not willing to do something concrete and constructive about it, in his own family and out in society.

Conclusion: Only if the woman is liberated can the family survive. The man in the family has to become just as much of a resource for the woman, as the woman is for the man.

Now then, if we take up this gauntlet which Berit Ås and many others have thrown down — and in my opinion we should do that — then we in industry should ask ourselves the following question: Looking ahead, how can we create such conditions that the fathers not only get the opportunity to, but actually become motivated to be at home as "househusbands" a substantial part of their time, while the holes thereby being created in the outside work force are filled by qualified women? How can we realistically start such a process?

Norway has, of course, made great strides in that direction in the intervening decades.

In another article entitled "Cultural Revolution," Knut asked what it would take for privileged society to "reduce our wasteful extravagant consumption" and "get in contact with other qualities of life more valuable than the materialistic." The article focused on the responsibility of rich countries to deal with the realities of the developing world — hunger, suffering, poverty, sickness and overpopulation. He quoted Maurice Strong: "The root of all ills sits in the materialistic and competition driven attitudes, dominating our whole culture." We must get a social system, Strong is quoted as saying, that places "the economy" in its rightful place, "at the service of social goals." Such statements, Knut writes, are not easily pushed under the carpet, pretending that they have not been heard. Maybe we *do* need a cultural revolution, he suggests.

Being a down-to-earth "friend of man" and a contributing member of his community is every bit as important in Knut's life as his international business ventures spanning many decades and several continents. "Think globally but act locally" is a concept, attributed to René Dubos (acting as an advisor to the United Nations Conference on the Human Environment in 1972), which suggests that global problems can turn into action only by considering ecological, economic and cultural differences of our local surroundings. In 1979, Dubos suggested that ecological consciousness should begin at home. He believed that there needed to be a creation of a World Order in which "natural and social units maintain or recapture their identity, yet interplay with each other through a rich system of communications." In the 1980's, Dubos held to his thoughts on acting locally and felt that issues involving the environment must be dealt with in their "unique physical, climatic and cultural contexts" (*The Encyclopedia of the Environment*, Eblen & Eblen, 1994).

Action at the individual and local level is the first step any of us can take in trying to help improve our communal future. Knut Utstein Kloster believes that the decisions we make, and the actions we take, here and now, right at home, will affect the planet we pass on to future generations. It was for this reason that, throughout his life, he never turned his back on the problems in his community and the challenges right at home in his backyard. That community heart is a measure of a person's true concern for the larger problems facing society and the planet.

Knut in the woods with his best friend, Kahnin.

CHAPTER ELEVEN
Staying Grounded

Knut believes that a world view is not inconsistent with local interests, national pride and treasuring one's cultural heritage. Many of his activities and accomplishments relate to his Norwegian roots and to shipping.

Throughout his life, Knut has been an active and contributing member of society in Norway. He was Chairman of the Oslo Shipowner's Association and Vice Chairman of the Norwegian Journal of Trade and Shipping. In working with the Norwegian Shipowners' Association, Knut chaired several important committees, including one which established a nationwide network of "study groups" and another that was responsible for handling the Association's liaison with society, media policies, educational programs and general industry outreach to foster public understanding of the importance of the shipping industry to the country.

Knut also served as chairman of the Red Cross Building Committee to create an allergy institute in Norway. He pioneered and chaired the planning, design, financing and organization of a residential and service facility for seniors. He sponsored a phonographic record, "Stars on Norway," with Norwegian actress Liv

Ullmann, Norwegian broadcaster Erik Bye and many contributing performers in support of a catastrophic fund for world refugees.

He initiated NORSHOW, the Norwegian (Gateway to Scandinavia) pavilion at Epcot Center. He organized and implemented an educational program on shipping for the country's maritime schools and participated in creating the Norwegian Shipping Academy. Knut also initiated and promoted a Norwegian organization for seamen's wives to help them better cope with their husbands' long absences. (In those days, most Norwegian crew were men, but today, many women have taken up the call of the sea.)

Knut represented the shipping industry in LIBERTAS, a national cross-industry organization dedicated to the cause of protecting free enterprise "from creeping socialist encroachment" through a continuous process of providing the public and elected officials information "showing how important free enterprise is in protecting and preserving freedom generally."

He was active in mobilizing community responsibility against juvenile delinquency by creating youth residences, special schools, humanitarian organizations and clubs to help young people in need. He served on the board of the Norwegian Family Council, dedicated to developing three generational housing projects; he organized hiking programs for school children where they could learn to read maps and use the compass. And he actively supported crisis centers and animal shelters.

Tage Wandborg tells a story about Knut that goes back to 1966 when they were planning for the construction of the *M/S SUNWARD*. A business conference was in session at Klosters Rederi A/S, but Knut was interrupted by his secretary to say that a Norwegian prisoner was on the telephone, asking to speak with him. Knut had been a regular visitor to the local prison under the auspices of the Red Cross. He had told the prisoners to feel free and call him at any time, day or night, if they needed to speak with him. So when one actually did, he naturally took the call.

Knut also started and chaired the establishment of Industritjeneste A/S — an industrial service enterprise offering jobs to released prisoners who needed a foothold to get back into society.

All of Knut's contributions to shipping and the cruise industry, and his commitment to sustainability, a healthier planet and a better world for all children, accrue in many ways to Norway where his globalist values were born and nurtured.

A few years ago, Knut was awarded the highest honor that can be bestowed on a Norwegian — the Order of St. Olav. Knut received the award for his contribution to the shipping industry in Norway. He felt very uncomfortable about the award, believing that no one person, but rather all the men and women who have contributed to Norway's shipping industry, should receive such an award. He accepted it only on the basis that it was intended to recognize the contributions of all involved in Norway's important shipping industry.

Norwegian school children are joined by British scientist, James Lovelock, his wife Sandy, and Knut Kloster onboard GAIA at Sandefjord.

The Vinland Revisited expedition (Chapter Six) started out as a Norwegian-Icelandic project but expanded when *GAIA* the Viking ship was sent on from Washington to Rio and the Earth Summit. Knut's initial investment involved the acquisition of the replica Viking ship, *GAIA*, and costs associated with her journey to Vinland (America). It was Norway's spirit of discovery that motivated the expedition and Knut's participation in the project. He saw how — in today's world — that spirit of discovery could be directed toward discovering better ways to live together in harmony with one another and with Mother Earth. At the end of the *GAIA* to Rio voyage, Knut donated the ship to the municipality of Sandefjord, the location in Norway where the original Gogstad Viking ship was excavated, and she is well cared for there, enjoyed throughout the year by the children and "grown-ups" of the region.

Knut renamed the *S/S FRANCE* the *S/S NORWAY* (Chapter Three), and the ship immediately became part of the country's national heritage. In the summer of 1984, the *S/S NORWAY* visited her adopted homeland. It was an exhilarating cruise up and down Norway's long rugged coastline to the North Cape and the "land of the midnight sun." That was a momentous occasion for Norwegians. Thousands of citizens gathered along her route in the towns and villages visited, in and out of Norway's many beautiful fjords, and to Oslo, the nation's capital. A virtual flotilla of small- and medium-sized boats accompanied the ship everywhere she went.

In a wonderful book written about the *S/S Norway* and this historic visit,[20] the authors recounted the ship's call at the ancient Hanseatic City of Bergen: "A reigning monarch could not have been given a more enthusiastic welcome," they wrote.

---

[20] *S.S. NORWAY* — A Tribute in Words and Pictures — published by Forlaget Nordvest (1984/85)

When it was announced that the 1994 Winter Olympics would be held in Norway, Knut was determined to join his fellow countrymen and women to make the event the best it could possibly be. Most importantly, Norwegians wanted to share with the world as much as possible about their country, its history, culture, spirit of discovery and commitment to nature and the environment.

Norway recognized that the '94 Winter Olympics (OL-94) would be its most significant international event of the decade. Since Norway is often thought of as "an environmental nation" and its Prime Minister at the time, Hon. Gro Harlem Brundtland, was often referred to as "the world's environment minister,"[21] Norway recognized that it had a special responsibility and opportunity to make the '94 Winter Olympics an environmental showcase. Norway

---

[21]Hon. Gro Harlem Brundtland served as chairman of the UN World Commission on Environment and Development which led to the 1992 Earth Summit.

has long encouraged international agreements for protection of the environment and for sustainable development, and the organizing committee realized that the eyes of the world would now be focused on Norway's own environment and environmental policies, all the more so as a nation rich in natural resources.

The aim was an "environmentally friendly Olympics" with special attention directed at the construction of environmentally responsible buildings as well as infrastructure development that served the purpose of the Games while preserving the natural environment and having a constructive useful life for Norwegian citizens when the Games were over.

Knut undertook the single largest construction project associated with the Olympics' development — creation of Hafjell village where the global media would be housed during the Olympics at Lillehammer. Again, Knut invoked Gaia, Mother Earth, as the theme of the project. Hafjell was to be a traditional Norwegian village — a twenty-minute drive from the center of Lillehammer and a short walk to the top of the Olympic slalom and downhill ski trails as well as some of Norway's most treasured cross-country skiing and hiking trails. Hafjell was comprised of 225 traditional sod-roofed cottages — in designs dating back centuries — and 125 apartments plus a large community center, Gaiastova, which would be home base to the world's media during the events. Knut arranged to have the original Robert McCall[22] "floating city" oil painting, which he had commissioned to depict *PHOENIX WORLD CITY*, hung at Gaiastova during the event.

---

[22] Robert McCall is America's foremost space artist whose vision of the future has inspired over 400 paintings and murals. Over ten million people a year admire his massive six-story high mural of man's landing on the moon, at the entrance of the National Air and Space Museum in Washington, D.C. Isaak Asimov describes McCall as "the closest thing we have to an artist-in-residence in outer space." McCall has a series of paintings entitled "floating cities" which depict futuristic cities in space. His painting of *PHOENIX WORLD CITY* is entitled "Voyage into the Future."

After the Olympics, the cottages and apartments were sold to private individuals and corporations. Today, many Norwegian families come to Hafjell to enjoy the sweeping views of the mountains and the Gudbransdalen Valley below and to enjoy hiking, cross-country and downhill skiing, as well as great memories of the '94 Olympics. Hafjell was one of the most successful development projects associated with the event.

In Chapter Five, *Hands Across the Sea*, Knut's city-ship project was sent abroad for further development and realization in a country which generates over 90% of cruise revenues and which would enable the project to take advantage of additional markets such as coastwise trading and meetings and conferences. Nonetheless, to the extent that the American Flagship project would rely on foreign technology, Knut requested that Norwegian technology be given a preference. "Hands across the sea" was to work both ways, to the extent that Norway — one of the leading maritime nations of the world — could provide products and services that are not available, or as competitively available, in the United States. In this spirit of cooperation, over $100 million worth of Norwegian products and services have been specified for the American Flagship and Letters of Intent have been entered into to formalize this cooperation. Among the Norwegian companies to benefit from participation in the American Flagship project are Jets Vacuum AS, York-Novenco AS, Autronica Fire and Security AS, Rapp Bomek AS, Norsk Inova AS, Vincard AS, and NORAC AS.

In May of 1981, Knut was given a plaque by the Sons of Norway for his dedication and service as a member of the Advisory Board. The Sons of Norway was originally organized in 1895 as a fraternal benefit society by 18 Norwegian immigrants in Minneapolis, Minnesota. The purposes and goals of the Founding Fathers were to protect members of Sons of Norway and their families from the financial hardships experienced during times of sickness or death in the family. Over time, the mission of Sons of Norway was expanded to include the preservation and celebration of Norwegian heritage and culture. It is the largest Norwegian organization outside Norway.

Faithful family fjord horse or brave lion symbol?

The national symbol of Norway has for centuries been a lion. Norway's national shield depicts a golden lion standing upright on his hind legs with a crown on his head and holding up a silver axe. Two lions mark the entrance to the Norwegian Parliament Building in Oslo to protect the members.

Some Norwegians, including Knut, proposed that a more meaningful and appropriate national symbol for Norway should be the Norwegian fjord horse. It is believed that the original fjord horse migrated to Norway and was domesticated over 4,000 years ago. It is a hardy, adaptable and efficient breed; calm and gentle, yet active and gregarious. When asked why the fjord horse would be a more meaningful and appropriate national symbol, Knut said:

> This frugal and persevering small horse has played a very important role through hard and difficult times in bringing the Norwegian people to where we are today. Out on the farms, especially in the rugged western part of the country, the fjord horse was part of the family in a very real sense. The horse is strong enough for heavy work, such as plowing the fields or pulling timber, yet light and fast enough to be a good riding and driving horse. There are many sweet stories about how the family's fjord horse was participating in bringing up the children...teaching them to ride and sit tight, purposely going under a branch that would make the child fall off if he or she

wasn't alert and careful; and with the whole family deeply moved at the end, saying goodbye to their beloved friend.

Today, the fjord horse is a favorite at Norwegian riding and therapeutic schools as its generally mild temperament and small size make it suitable for children and disabled individuals.

Not so long ago, Norway was one of the poorest countries in Europe, and life for most people was really tough. We owe a huge debt to the fjord horse and, in many people's view, it should be our national symbol rather than the lion with which we have no real or actual connection.

This fjord horse anecdote tells quite a bit about Knut Utstein Kloster: down-to-earth, practical, seeing and appreciating simple realities, and proposing a national symbol that has some true meaning and significance for the country — the hard-working gentle fjord horse versus the mythical protective lion.

One of Knut's good friends was the late Erik Bye[23], the prominent Norwegian journalist. Erik Bye wrote a story about Norwegian immigration to America, *Blow, Silver Wind.* With the exception of Ireland, no single country has contributed a larger percentage of her population to America than Norway. Bye's story begins in 1825 with the sailing of the first "immigrant vessel", the sloop *RESTAURATION,* from Stavanger to New York. The story ends with a salute to the *S.S. NORWAY,* also en route to New York, after her triumphant 1984 visit to her adopted homeland. In wishing her 'god seilas' (a happy voyage), Bye writes:

---

[23] Erik Bye was a much revered man not only in Norway but also in America where he spent many years. In 2008, a film was released in Norway, GIGANTEN (Giant) about Bye's life and contributions as a journalist, author, poet, producer, broadcaster...and exemplar. A chieftain in Norway's cultural life.

She represents the strong bonds between our countries that have existed ever since the *RESTAURATION* made her historic crossing in 1825.

In Bye's story, he suggests that Knud Rasmussen Kloster, our Knut's ancestor, was no doubt present in the crowd that day when the *RESTAURATION* set sail for the New World: "He belonged to an old seafaring family, and it makes sense that his descendents later established their shipping company in that very city."

Hence, the bond between Knut and Norway, Knut and America, and Knut and what he calls "no man's land,"[24] is easy to trace and admire.

---

[24] Knut's "no man's land" is defined as "the distance between the world-*that-is* and the world-*as-it-should be.*"

CHAPTER TWELVE
The Future Belongs to Those Who Take It...

In one of his 1976 articles for *KAPITAL,* Knut talked about "Vår fremtid", our future:

> I think it was Aldous Huxley, the British author, who once remarked: "A fact remains a fact even if you choose to ignore it." The fact we are facing today, which increasingly will set the stage for developing countries in years to come, is that they will no longer accept the rules of the game set by the "elite class of nations." These rules have stamped the economic and trade political development over the last 500 years ever since Vasco da Gama gave Europe a footing in Africa and India and up until the fall of 1973 when the counter wave came from the OPEC countries. The rules of the game are now in the melting pot; they will surely be radically changed as time moves on. ***

> The sooner we get started with the process of leveling the field between rich and poor countries, the better it will be for the development of a healthy world trade. *** I think we ought to engage ourselves actively, industry-wise, in the process of setting the stage for the development of a new economic global system — a system which will challenge our traditional thinking by giving the great majority of the world's people a concrete experience, at long last, of getting a "fair deal."

It was Adlai Stevenson, back in 1953, who said that the future belongs to those to take it. A half century later, we know that if we do not take hold of the future, it will take hold of us.

Knut has always seen clearly that a "fair deal" for every man, woman and child on the planet is the only path to peace and prosperity. He has seen that Mother Nature demands nothing less than that from her inhabitants — a fair deal: that we share her bounty, respect her rules, preserve her natural resources, protect the delicate balance between air, water, land and life, and give back more than we take from her during our time on Earth.

Each of us, of course, must follow our own light, our own star, our own inner compass. But we share a common future — or a common fate. Knut's story shows how we can use our time, talents, experience, business ventures and knowledge — our hearts and our heads — to take hold of the future and steer a healthier, more equitable, and sustainable course forward. When asked about the "flickering soul" metaphor, used in his 1981 speech at the Norwegian-American Chamber of Commerce (Chapter Eight), which is used in the sub-title of the book, Knut wrote:

> In Norwegian, it is "flakkende sjel." I just looked up "flakkende" in the dictionary, and there it was, "flickering." "Sjel" and "soul" was easy. So there it is, flickering soul. And it *does* hurt. I wonder if it isn't how billions of people around the world feel, when you get right down to what it means to be a human being. Whether you are so-called rich or poor. No man's land is where you are, in your heart and mind, and/or between right and left, and/or in believing or not believing in the divine creation, wanting to do the right thing — but overwhelmed by the enormity of the challenge.

We can't "stop the world" because we want to "get off" — to borrow from the popular 1966 Broadway musical. But we can make a difference. We can help create a better future. It is not a matter of being a big financial success, making a big splash, or how often one is seen in the media. But rather, using the opportunities we have and the work we are doing to help bridge that huge gap between the world-*as-it-is* and the world-*as-it-should-be*. That is what Knut Utstein Kloster has done his entire life. We possess the scientific and technological resources to solve the world's problems and to construct a positive future for all its citizens. The challenge of our time is to find ways to apply these resources to basic human needs on a global scale and to integrate scientific and technological advances with human values and global ethics. Millions of individuals and organizations and institutions around the world are devoted to this task.

Knut Utstein Kloster is just one flickering soul, one candle in the dark, one star in the firmament. His projects — those which have been realized and those that will be realized in the future — are all examples of how every step we take can merge practical and idealistic objectives. We can all make a difference simply by caring and following our own True North.

EPILOGUE

"In life we find many men that are great, and some that are good, but very few men are both great and good."
— Charles Caleb Colton

I was motivated to write this book because I had the pleasure and privilege of knowing such a man.

In 2007, the Cruise Line International Association (CLIA), North America's cruise industry organization, honored Knut by inducting him into the Hall of Fame as a pioneer of the cruise industry. In accepting the award for him, I spoke of Knut's less known pioneering in another field — the field of "doing well by doing good." I talked about his vision for the cruise industry and how it might play an important role in helping to shape a better future, particularly in terms of protecting the environment. I said that Knut hopes the ships of the future will become high profile examples of new energy-efficient technologies and as learning platforms where its passengers can enjoy their vacations along with increased awareness of, and participation in, programs and projects aimed at improving themselves and the world around them. The approximately 2,000 delegates attending CLIA's Hall of Fame event, consisting mostly of travel agents (the backbone of the cruise industry), seemed to embrace the message. It was a good night and I was extremely proud of Knut for his impact on the industry — past, present, and future.

Left to right: Andrew Stuart, Executive Vice President, Sales and Passenger Services for Norwegian Cruise Line; Stephanie Gallagher; Brad Anderson, Co-President of America's Vacation Center; Terry Dale, President of CLIA

AUTHOR'S NOTE

"And he shall judge among the nations, and shall rebuke many people: and they shall beat their swords into plowshares, and their spears into pruning hooks: nation shall not lift up sword against nation, neither shall they learn war any more."
— Isaiah 2:4

Before letting my kind readers go on now to their next engagement, I wish to share one final story about my subject, Knut Utstein Kloster. It was actually a chapter in the book (*GAIASHIP* — Coming Together as One World) which I removed when the publisher commented that it was "over the top" to be reading about another ship-of-the-future, however noble. The publisher further commented that the name given to the ship, *GAIASHIP*, was too confusing having just read about *GAIA* the Viking ship.

But Knut remains captivated by his *GAIASHIP* concept[1] — a ship that would travel the world, represent all nations, and have as her

---

[1] In developing the *GAIASHIP* concept, Knut collaborated with fellow Norwegian, Roar Bjerknes, a professional journalist and former Information Manager for GECO (geophysical exploration) and Oceanor (marine environment monitoring technology). Mr. Bjerknes spent many years in Asia and has been a strong proponent of cross-cultural communication throughout his career.

mission simply bringing people together to search for solutions to humankind's biggest problems. He saw the ship as a messenger of peace and a mediator of disputes between countries and cultures. He envisioned a UN flag flying on the ship, with the flags of all nations of the world also represented. Knut asked Tage Wandborg to design such a ship and the result is *GAIASHIP*.

The *GAIASHIP* concept was endorsed by the late eminent scientist, writer, and futurist, Sir Arthur C. Clarke, who wrote in a letter to Knut:

> I think it is an excellent idea — a proposal of global significance — the kind of collaborative international venture that our world needs now more than ever. *** There is nothing like a ship voyage to create a feeling of unity, as well as a better understanding of the wonderful planet on which we live. This would be an investment for a more peaceful future for all of us.

The proposed *GAIASHIP* is 767 feet long, carrying 1,072 passengers and an international crew of 520. The Gaia Globe, in the center of the ship — reminiscent of Planet Earth as seen from outer space — is the ship's signature attribute. The Gaia Globe would serve as a joint reminder of our global interdependence and the frailty of our Planet Earth. The World Future Society (WFS) also endorsed the concept and the ship was featured in The Futurist[2], a magazine published by the Society. In a letter of support from Edward Cornish, President of the Society, he writes:

> The World Future Society (WFS) strongly and unreservedly endorses the aims of the *GAIASHIP* as presented to us,

---

[2] *The Futurist* – Vol. 36, No. 6

and fully supports the proposed joint activity between the WFS and the Sir Arthur C. Clarke Foundation on board the vessel.

At present, over 90 percent of WFS activities take place within the United States. However, the Society has now declared its intention to become much more international in its operations: to become a World Future Society in effect as well as in name.

We believe that *GAIASHIP* could be the ideal vehicle to carry the WFS message to the rest of the world. We also see the vessel as a highly suitable base for our annual conferences, seminars and other events.

The World Future Society sees every benefit from the realization of the *GAIASHIP* Project, and is happy to join Sir Arthur in recommending it to all.

A future studies center is also planned, in collaboration the World Future Society and The Arthur C. Clarke Foundation. The center will be named in honor of Sir Arthur C. Clarke.

Knut believes that *GAIASHIP* should be financed, built and operated by oil rich Norway. "Not that long ago," says Knut, "Norway was one of the poorest countries in Europe. Today it is one of the richest, thanks to oil. Our national fortune per capita is immense. In a global perspective, sponsoring the creation of *GAIASHIP* by Norway, for the benefit of the United Nations and world peace, would be a good investment, pure and simple."

The point, of course, is not whether the government of Norway can be persuaded to support the "peace ship" initiative, but rather, what we all can do, following the excellent example of Knut Utstein Kloster, to stay focused on the possible, to seize every opportunity for good, and to follow our own True North.

Illustration of GAIASHIP globe by Terje Olsen

PHOTO CREDITS

Cover: Vintage Compass, Oleksandr Staroseltsev (Ukraine)

Page 73:   Westin/World City press conference, Janet Durrans (NY)

Page 91:   Tage Wandborg and Knut Utstein Kloster at Westin/World City press conference, Janet Durrans (NY)

Page 112: *GAIA's* helm with Sugar Loaf Mountian in the background, Andreas Valentin (Brazil)

Page 112: Insert of GAIA's arrival in Rio, Enrico Feroelli (NY)

Page 170: *S/S NORWAY* on visit to Norway, surrounded by flotilla, Fjellanger Wideroe

INDEX

Breinigsville, PA USA
30 September 2009
224967BV00003B/2/P